SPECIAL TIME

The Science of Marriage

Contents

Parts of this edition appeared previously in TIME, Health, Real Simple *or* Money.

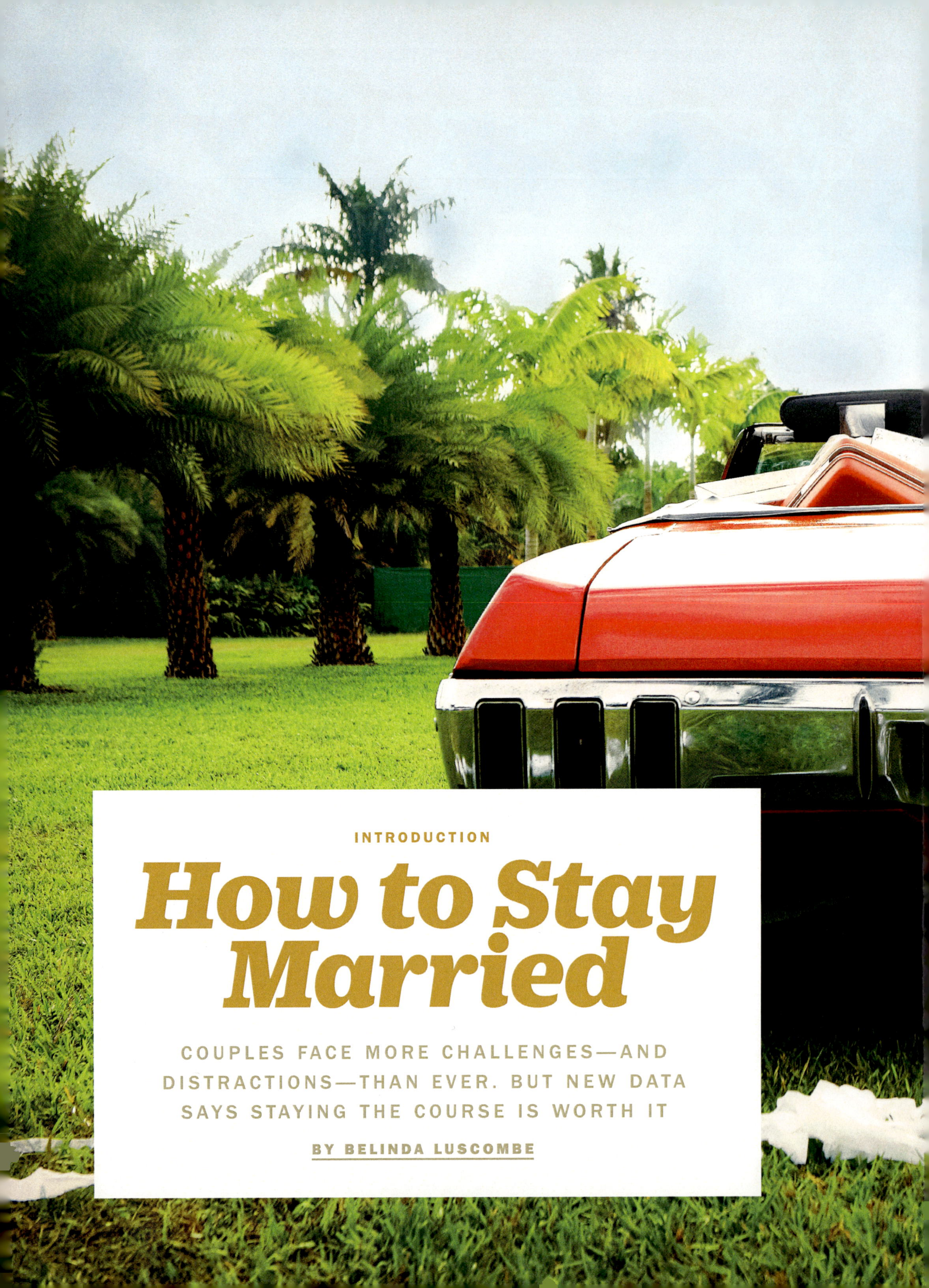

INTRODUCTION

How to Stay Married

COUPLES FACE MORE CHALLENGES—AND DISTRACTIONS—THAN EVER. BUT NEW DATA SAYS STAYING THE COURSE IS WORTH IT

BY BELINDA LUSCOMBE

There's a reason fairy tales always end in marriage. It's because nobody wants to see what comes after. It's too grim. Meeting the right person, working through comic misunderstandings and overcoming family disapproval to get to the altar—those are stories worth telling. Plodding on year after year with that same old soul? Yawnsville.

Most Americans still want to get married—even millennials, although they're waiting until they're older. To aid them in their search, businesses have devoted billions of dollars and thousands of gigabytes to mate-seeking. Lawyers have spent countless hours arguing that people should be able to marry whomever they choose, of any gender. Techies have refined recommendation engines so that people can more accurately find their perfect other half. In many ways, getting married is now easier than it has ever been.

But staying married, and doing so happily, is more difficult. In 2014, having spent a year looking at all the sociological, psychological, economic and historic data he could get his hands on, Northwestern University psychology professor Eli Finkel announced that marriage is currently both the most and the least satisfying the institution has ever been. "Americans today have elevated their expectations of marriage and can in fact achieve an unprecedentedly high level of marital quality," he writes, but only if they invest a lot of effort. And if they can't, their marriage will be more disappointing to them than a humdrum marriage was to prior generations, because they've been promised so much more.

Matrimony used to be an institution people entered out of custom, duty or a need to procreate. Now that it's become a technology-assisted endeavor that has been delayed until conditions are at their most optimal, it needs to deliver better-quality benefits. More of us think this one relationship should—and could—provide the full buffet of satisfaction: intimacy, support, stability, happiness and sexual exhilaration. And if it's not up to the task, it's quicker and cheaper than ever to unsubscribe. It's not clear any relationship can overcome that challenge.

It's not even clear anymore exactly what couples are signing up for. Marriage is the most basic and intimate of our social institutions but also the one most subject to shifts in cultural, technological and economic forces, many of which have made single life a completely viable and attractive proposition.

At the same time, new evidence keeps piling up that few things are as good for life, limb and liquidity as staying married. "Couples who have made it all the way later into life have found it to be a peak experience, a sublime experience to be together," says Karl Pillemer, a Cornell University gerontologist who did an intensive survey of 700 elderly people for his book *30 Lessons for Loving*. "Everybody—100%—said at one point that the long marriage was the best thing in their lives. "But all of them also either said that marriage is hard," he adds, "or that it's really, really hard."

Marriage has become what game theorists call "a commitment device," an undertaking that locks individuals into a course of action they might find dreary and inconvenient on occasion in order to help them achieve a bonus later on. And in an era when it's both harder and less necessary to stay together, the trick is figuring out how to go the distance so you can reap the rich rewards.

What does a modern marriage promise that historical unions didn't? The ultimate dream: a partner who sees what you really are and not only accepts it but improves it. "The promise you make is not just to be faithful and true and to stay married but to try and bring out the best in each other," says Lisa Grunwald, who with her husband, Stephen Adler, put together a historical compendium of marriage, *The Marriage Book*, in 2015. "To try and

Evidence keeps piling up that few things are as good for life, limb and liquidity as staying married.

THE MARRIAGE SLUMP?

Fewer Americans are married today, largely because fewer young people are tying the knot

WHO'S STILL IN HIS OR HER FIRST MARRIAGE AT 46?

38% of those who didn't finish high school

54% of whites, Asians, Pacific Islanders and Native Americans

69% of college graduates

47% of blacks

51% of Hispanics (any race)

ADULTS 18 OR OLDER WHO ARE...

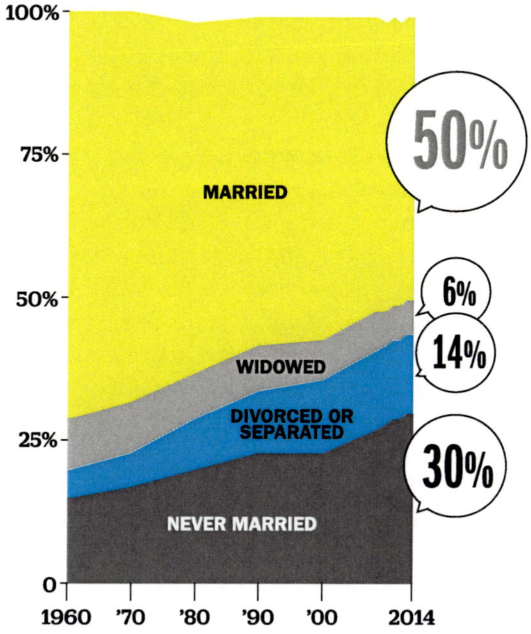

WHO'S STAYING MARRIED Women tend to stay in their first marriage if they get married after the age of 26 and the union is financially stable

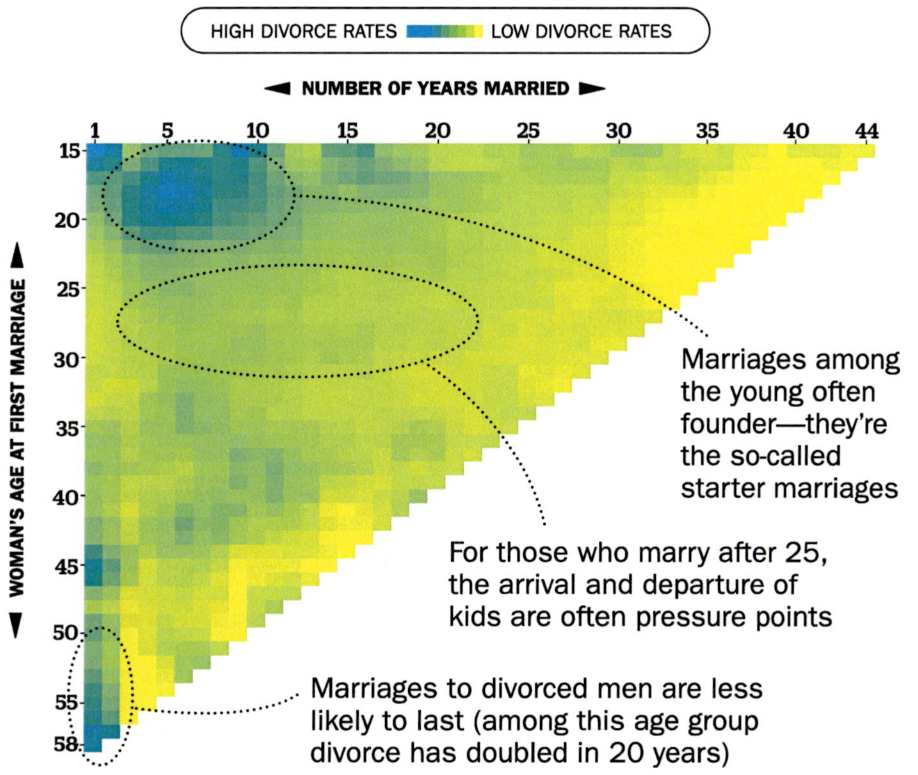

SOURCES: PEW; PHILIP N. COHEN, UNIVERSITY OF MARYLAND, USING 2011–13 AMERICAN COMMUNITY SURVEY DATA; BUREAU OF LABOR STATISTICS

understand, really deeply understand, what the other one wants and hold her feet or his feet to the fire and say, 'OK, this is great, but remember, this is what you wanted and don't let go of that dream.' "

And just as the benefits have changed, so have the challenges. The roles partners play in the home are a moving target. Child-rearing has long been discounted as the main reason for marrying, yet married couples today are encouraged to engage in it more intensively than before. Technology offers more enticements to stray while the culture and the law offer fewer penalties for doing so.

In some cases, the penalty is for staying. That Hillary Clinton stuck with a philandering husband is considered in some circles to be a liability, evidence of weakness or that the marriage is a sham. And when, in 2016, Beyoncé dropped *Lemonade*, her gloriously enraged album about infidelity, many people assumed that as a feminist she would soon be single. Not so. "Today, choosing to stay when you can leave is the new shame," says relationship therapist Esther Perel.

Beyoncé has plenty of time to change her mind; "until death do us part" is a much longer stretch than it used to be. People can get married, have kids, put them through college, retire and still have decades of life together ahead of them. For some, that's just way too much time with the one person with the one set of stories and gross habits. "Being married is like sharing a basement with a fellow hostage; after five years there are very few off-putting things you won't know about each other," writes Tim Dowling in *How to Be a Husband*. "After 10 years there are none." After 25 years, he might have added, you're ready to put his or her eyes out.

Opting out

So while divorce rates have been dropping among most age groups since the 1980s, there's one exception: older people. Divorce rates among this group are up. A report in 2014 found they have doubled among people 50 or older in the past two decades; more men over 55 are divorced than widowed. Only a tenth of the people who divorced in 1990 were over 50. In 2010, it was 25%. Some of those were in second or third marriages, which tend to be less stable than the first, but more than half of them were first-timers.

Some demographers have hypothesized that the reason marriage is most popular among the highly educated is that they see it as the optimal way to give advantage to their offspring. Unhappy couples often split at a later stage because they've waited until their kids have left: the empty-nest divorce. But it may be that it was the demands of child-rearing that first caused the rift. "If you look at time-use studies, all parents are spending more time with their children than parents with equivalent resources did decades ago," says University of California, Santa Barbara, demographer Shelly Lundberg. "And at the top end, among college graduates, we're definitely at a new level." Children are not merely fed, educated and sheltered; they are curated or, as family scholars put it, raised using "concerted cultivation."

This intensive parenting is made more complicated when both spouses work outside the home, as more do than even 20 years ago. Since the child-care burden is still primarily shouldered by women, they are often the more stressed partner. In addition, their careers make it simpler for them to imagine a life without a spouse. They have their own income, a network of friends and associates, and their own retirement savings.

And when people go home after work, their networks go with them. Social media has made it much easier to seek support and conversation elsewhere than in a spouse. Conveniently, it has also made it much easier to line up a new one if all that not-talking takes a toll. "Man is basically as faithful as his options," says noted marriage counselor/comedian Chris Rock. "No more, no less." And now people—of both sexes—feel like they have options to spare. They can find old

Since the 1980s, divorce rates have been dropping among all age groups—except older people.

flames easily. Or they can drop their lure into the vast schools of partners in online dating pools. Singledom looks less like murky waters and more like limpid ocean.

The good divorce

All of this would be academic, of course, without a reasonably unobstructed route to Splitsville. Divorce may feel like a failure, but it has lost a lot of stigma, and hassle. Since 2010, every state in the nation has allowed people to leave their spouses without accusing them of anything—and in most states, it doesn't even require their consent. Mediators are making divorce cheaper and less onerous. There are self-help books, TV shows and websites dedicated to the once unthinkable concept of the good divorce, what practitioners Gwyneth Paltrow and Chris Martin popularized as "conscious uncoupling."

Lifetime monogamy, as many have pointed out, is not a natural state. Very few animals mate for life, and most of those that do are either birds or really ugly (Malagasy giant rat, anyone?). One theory as to why humans took to monogamy is that it strengthens societies by reducing competition among males.

But natural and worthwhile are not the same things. Reading isn't a natural thing to do. Neither is painting, snowboarding or coding. But nobody suggests we abandon those pursuits. Monogamy also has a certain energy-saving appeal: it saves humans from wasting time and effort on constantly hunting for new mates or recovering from betrayals by current ones.

For those who can stay the course, indicators that a long marriage is worth the slog continue to mount. Studies suggest that married people have better health, wealth and even better sex lives than their single counterparts, and will probably die happier.

Healthier and wealthier

It's also possible, researchers propose, that individuals who share wealth and expenses can afford superior health care. The couple's well-being might actually not be due to their marriage but because those whose finances are in order are more likely to get married in the first place.

In later life, your relationship becomes very much like it was during your courtship.

Even so, married women's finances are generally more robust than divorced women's. "Historically, divorced women have had the highest poverty rates among all-aged women in the United States," says Barbara Butrica, a labor economist at the Urban Institute.

Of course, money isn't the only thing women need. There's also sex. A 2011 Kinsey Institute study of sexual satisfaction in the U.S., Germany, Spain, Brazil and Japan found that women in committed relationships were feeling more sexually satisfied after 15 years together than they were in the first decade and a half of the relationship.

John Gottman, one of the nation's leading marriage researchers and educators, reports that older married couples tend to behave like younger married couples outside the bedroom too. "The surprising thing is that the longer people are together, the more the sense of kindness returns," he reports. "Our research is starting to reveal that in later life, your relationship becomes very much like it was during courtship."

The kid connection

The biggest disincentive to divorce, however, may be the same as one of the biggest drivers of divorce: kids. Many sociologists and therapists agree that kids from what are known as "intact marriages," as a whole, do better on most fronts than kids from divorced families, unless the marriage is very high-conflict. (It should be noted that therapists are clear that some marriages are just too toxic to sustain, and if a spouse is in physical danger, he or she must leave.) Not all children of divorce are the walking wounded their whole lives, but the stats are not encouraging.

Research suggests that in the long term, children of divorced parents are more at risk of being poor, being unhealthy, having mental illness, not graduating from college and get-

ting divorced themselves. It's true that being poor might be the cause of all the other adversities. Nevertheless, studies that have taken income into account still found that kids from divorced families face more challenges than those from parents who stayed married.

The things we don't know about what keeps people together are legion. But here are some of the things we do know: If people get married after about the age of 26, have college degrees, haven't already had kids or gotten pregnant, and are gainfully employed, they tend to stay married. If individuals form romantic partnerships with individuals who are similar to them in values and background, they find it easier to stay married. And the devout, by a slim but significant margin, get divorced slightly less often than people for whom faith is not a big deal.

But what's the trick once you're hitched? It's hard to do thorough scientific testing of what actually makes a marriage work, because of the ethics of experimenting with people's lives, but over the years, sociologists, psychologists and therapists have seen patterns emerging.

One constant is to avoid contempt at all costs. By contempt, therapists mean more than making derogatory remarks about a partner's desirability or earning power. It's also communicated by constant interruption, dismissal of their concerns or withdrawal from conversation.

Contempt, say therapists, sets off a lethal chain reaction. It kills vulnerability, among other things. Vulnerability is a prerequisite for intimacy. Without intimacy, commitment is a grind. And without commitment, the whole enterprise goes pear-shaped.

Alas, contempt's favorite condition for breeding is familiarity. And you can't have a family without familiarity.

How to avoid it? There are two main antidotes, says Gary Chapman, arguably the country's most successful marriage therapist—his book *The 5 Love Languages* has been on some version of the *New York Times* best-seller list for eight straight years. The first, obvious as it sounds, is to figure out what specifically makes your partner feel loved. (According to Chapman, it's probably one of five things: words, time, kindly acts, sex or gifts.) And the other is to learn to apologize and to forgive. Disagreements are inevitable and healthy, so learning to fight fair is essential; resentment is one of contempt's chief co-conspirators.

Going the distance

Obvious idea that actually works No. 2 is to find shared interests, which can help offset the changes that relationships go through. "The most successful couples began to embrace one another's interests," says Pillemer. Since people are staying healthy longer, they can be active much longer. "We try to find everything we can think of that we really like to do together," Jimmy Carter has said, and his 70-year marriage to Rosalynn has endured four years in a governor's mansion, one presidency, several failed campaigns and a passion for Trikkes, among other trials.

Another helpful adjustment is to drop the idea of finding a soul mate. "We have this mythological idea that we will find a soul mate and have these euphoric feelings forever," says Chapman. In fact, soul mates tend to be crafted, not found. "There are tens of thousands of people out there that anyone could be happily married to," says Gottman, "and each marriage would be different."

And how do you make a soul mate? Practice, practice, practice. Pillemer observed that long-married couples he had interviewed always acted as if divorce were not an option. "People really had the mind-set they wanted to stay married," he says. They regarded their partnership as less like buying a new car and more like learning to drive. "Marriage is like a discipline," he says. "A discipline is not reaching one happy end point."

If all that discipline sounds a bit dreary, take heart, because the regimen includes bedroom calisthenics. A 2015 study found that sex once a week was the optimum amount for maximizing marital happiness. A group of Canadian researchers who analyzed data from three different studies found that sex played an even bigger role than money in happiness. The difference in life satisfaction between couples who had sex once a week and those who had it less than once a month was bigger than the difference between those who had an annual income of $50,000 to $75,000 and those who had an annual income between $15,000 and $25,000.

Sex, of course, does not occur in a vacuum. Therapists urge couples not to let the kids keep them from going out. "It does not have to be huge swaths of time but bits or chunks," says Scott Stanley, a co-director of the Center for Marital and Family Studies at the University of Denver. "Even something as simple as taking a walk together after dinner." This is not a time to work out differences. "When they should be in fun-and-friendship mode, [some people] switch into problem and conflict mode. Don't mix modes."

One of the more controversial ideas therapists are now suggesting is that men need to do more of the "emotional labor" in a relationship—the work that goes into sustaining love—which usually falls to women. "What men do in a relationship is, by a large margin, the crucial factor that separates a great relationship from a failed one," writes Gottman in his book *The Man's Guide to Women*. "This doesn't mean that a woman doesn't need to do her part, but the data proves that a man's actions are the key variable that determines whether a relationship succeeds or fails."

The one piece of advice every expert and nonexpert gives for staying married is perhaps the least useful one for those who are already several years in: choose well. The cascade of hormones that rains down on humans when they first fall in love, while completely necessary and wonderful, can sometimes blind individuals to their poor choices. Therapists suggest you ask friends about your prospective life mate. Aim to find someone you know you'll love even during the periods when you don't like him or her so much.

And then cross your fingers. As Grunwald puts it in an aphorism that may end up in a future marriage book: "Just pick out a good one and get lucky."

CHAPTER 1:

LOVE &

Romance

All About Attraction

WHAT MAKES TWO PEOPLE CLICK? FALL IN LOVE? KEEP THAT SPARK LONG-TERM? BRAIN RESEARCH AND EVOLUTIONARY SCIENCE ARE PROVIDING FASCINATING ANSWERS

BY GINNY GRAVES

Like superheroes, every happily married duo has an origin story, and most of these how-we-met tales contain important nuggets of truth about the mysterious forces that draw two strangers, magnet-like, toward each other. Here's mine. I was at a softball field in San Francisco waiting for my teammates to arrive one crisp spring day in 1991, when a slim, 6′2″ guy with a glove in his hand trotted toward me. He looked like a young Gregory Peck and introduced himself as Gordon. His voice was deep, his smile dreamy. When I cracked a joke about his career in public relations, he not only got it, he threw his head back and laughed. The exchange took 90 seconds, tops. By the time he jogged away to go warm up, I was a goner.

Which qualities pulled me in? Gordon's handsome face, for sure. But based on dozens of studies over the past decade or so, it's likely that everything from his strong baritone (masculine!) to his height (half of all women will only date men who are taller than they are) to his laugh (a sign of geniality)—and maybe even his scent (more on this later)—was working its subconscious mojo to make my heart do cartwheels. "There are dozens of factors that attract you to one person and not another. Some we learn and others are probably embedded in our DNA—an artifact of evolution designed to encourage us to go forth and multiply," says Helen Fisher, a senior research fellow at the Kinsey Institute

and author of *Anatomy of Love: A Natural History of Mating, Marriage and Why We Stray.*

With roughly 90 million unmarried people between the ages of 20 and 60 in the U.S. (and about equal numbers of men and women), there are, in the time-tested vernacular of dating, a whole lot of fish in the sea. Many of them are darting around trying to find The One. But how do you catch someone's eye? And why are some couples able to sustain that intoxicating zing for a lifetime? Science is finally cracking the attraction code.

Hot or not? First impressions

Let's say you glimpse someone across a crowded room. It takes your brain about 100 milliseconds, according to a Princeton University study, to form judgments about a host of traits: attractiveness, likeability, trustworthiness, competence and aggressiveness. "That first moment is a key decision point: Will you engage with that person, or look for someone else?" says Fisher. It seems a little hasty. But we humans are walking billboards for who we are. Everything about your appearance—height, weight, body language, clothing—conveys data about your socioeconomic background, education level, health and even grooming habits, all of which are critical fodder for the brain's attraction algorithm.

Some elements of attraction are nearly universal and probably evolved over the millennia to help us identify healthy mating partners. We tend to gravitate to people who look robust, with clear skin and bright eyes (clues to potential fertility). Most of us are interested in people who come from backgrounds similar to our own and who have the same ballpark level of attractiveness and education. "And cleanliness is a surprisingly strong aspect of attraction across cultures," adds Fisher. A happy demeanor helps, too. Several years ago, Swiss researchers found that people rate pictures of the same face as more attractive when the person is smiling than when he or she has a neutral expression—and a joyful beam was enough to make the raters judge even relatively unattractive people favorably. "Smiling is a sign of healthy emotional adjustment and a good personality," says Fisher.

But those instantaneous assessments of potential partners aren't wholly governed by Mother Nature. They're also influenced by your unique history—what Fisher calls your "love map": an image of your ideal sweetheart you've been subconsciously sketching and revising, based on relationships with your parents, friends, crushes and exes, since you were a child. We all have a built-in bias for beauty, for instance. "The more symmetrical the face the more your brain finds it pleasing, possibly because symmetry is a Darwinian sign of good health," explains Fisher. But by the time we're in our 20s and 30s, our idea of what makes someone good looking has become more complex and personal. "We've learned that beauty is skin-deep, and we've met people we're wildly attracted to who don't fit the traditional mold," says Jim Pfaus, a professor of neuroscience and biology at Concordia University in Montreal.

Women vary, for instance, in their level of attraction to certain personality traits they see reflected in faces. Those who value honesty, warmth, cooperation and parenting skill seem to favor men with more feminized faces (fuller cheeks, narrower jaws), whereas someone looking for a dominant provider might be naturally drawn to guys with a square chin and prominent brow—signs of high testosterone. While men are more likely to go for women with traditionally feminine features—full lips, wide cheeks—Australian researchers reported in 2015 that, when looking at online dating profiles and describing their ideal partners, both men and women preferred noncomformists, meaning those whose clothes, opinions or life decisions broke the norm. "Being different can be extremely attractive," says Pfaus, "and it makes sense from an evolutionary perspective, because it helps us preserve diversity in the species."

And then there's smell. Animals can often discern age, gender, dominance status, health

We tend to gravitate to people who look robust, with clear skin and bright eyes (clues to potential fertility).

status and availability in a single sniff—and many species emit pheromones, chemicals that work as an aphrodisiac. Male boar saliva, for instance, gives off scents that cause fertile females to turn around and present their behinds. We can all be grateful that humans are not wired to do the same. "But there's no question that odors play at least a muted role in human sexual attraction," says Gary Beauchamp, the emeritus director and president of the Monell Chemical Senses Center in Philadelphia. For instance, we probably each have a unique odor fingerprint—individual scents we emit that are associated with a set of genes involved in immune function, known as major histocompatibility complex—and these odors may play a role in attraction. "Animals choose mates who are different, odor-wise, so their offspring have a varied immune repertoire to help them survive bacteria and viruses—and there's some indication this happens in humans, too," says Beauchamp. Indeed, research has shown that women prefer the scent of sweaty T-shirts worn by men with MHC genes dissimilar to their own.

But in order to smell people, you need to get close to them—which brings us back to that intriguing person across the room. If he or she is a reasonable likeness of the fantasy sweetheart in your mind's eye, a primitive area buried deep in your brain—the ventral tegmental area (VTA)—has probably already begun churning out dopamine, a neurochemical that boosts focus, energy and motivation. "The VTA is the brain's 'go!' system," says Fisher, and by giving you the neurological equivalent of liquid courage, yours is goading you to cross the room and say hi.

Lovers have rose-colored glasses

So you've been on a couple of successful dates, maybe even slept together, which means you've moved on to Stage 2: infatuation. Attraction can wane at any point during this process. (Maybe you're turned off by his constant texting or her disdain for your circle of friends.) If it doesn't, your brain is going to start not-so-subtly nudging you toward this person.

To understand how attraction deepens into love, scientists have turned to an improbable source: the prairie vole. These stout, mouse-like creatures are unremarkable in every way save one. They form pair bonds and mate for life, which makes them perfect for studying the neurochemical process that's happening when we meet someone and fall in love. And a lot of it has to do, perhaps not surprisingly, with sex.

"All mammals get a hit of dopamine when they have sex. That big hit of pleasure is what makes sex rewarding so you want to do it again and again," says Larry Young, a professor in the department of psychiatry at Emory University and author of *The Chemistry Between Us: Love, Sex and the Science of Attraction*. But after prairie voles copulate, their brains, unlike 97% of other mammals, also secrete oxytocin, a neurochemical that creates a heightened bond with that individual in particular. Humans, subsequent research shows, secrete this pro-monogamy hormone, too. "Oxytocin makes you pay attention to every detail of your partner—their smell, their voice, their face," says Young. "By pairing it with the pleasurable feeling of dopamine, your brain is conditioning itself to release oxytocin every time you hold hands with this person or look in her eyes."

The heady combination of dopamine and oxytocin is what makes you think about your new partner 24/7—and oxytocin even makes your new paramour look more attractive. In 2013, researchers in Germany showed 20 men in romantic relationships photos of their sweethearts, as well as pictures of strangers who had been vetted as equally attractive. The men rated each photo on a scale of 1 to 10. Then the researchers squirted oxytocin or a placebo into the men's noses and had them view the photos and rate them again. The men who had received oxytocin rated their partners' images as more attractive than before but gave strangers' photos the same score. The researchers' conclusion: Oxytocin is like beer goggles for lovebirds.

The secrets of long-term attraction

Three brain systems play a role in the arc of a love story: Your sex drive spurs you to look for a range of partners, dopamine-fueled romantic love focuses your mating energy on one person, and the oxytocin-driven attachment system encourages you to stay with your partner at least while raising children. It doesn't always work out, of course.

To determine why some couples remain deeply attracted, Fisher and her colleagues put test pairs in an fMRI brain scanner. All had adult children, and they had been married an average of 21 years, but their brains lit up like sweethearts who had just fallen happily in love. All three of those love-related systems were thriving. Fortunately, there are behaviors that can keep them alive.

First, it's critical to maintain your sex life, because orgasm leaves you intoxicated with dopamine, and postcoital snuggling releases oxytocin—which bonds you. "Lie there and marinate in the chemicals surging through your system," says Pfaus. "These moments are relationship glue."

Dopamine also gets a boost from novel activities—going to a fun, new restaurant for dinner, riding bikes, learning to scuba dive—says Fisher. Oxytocin flows when you stay in touch—literally—so walk arm in arm, kiss, hold hands, cuddle.

And about that origin story. How you tell it may be a powerful clue to the health of your relationship. In a landmark 1992 study, University of Washington researchers found they could predict with 94% accuracy which couples would divorce or stay together by hearing them relate the story of how they met. It didn't matter whether the story was mundane or movie-worthy. What mattered was this: that the twosome shared the tale with a sense of fondness and solidarity. So tell your story to anyone who will listen, including each other. Reminiscing about your shared history just might help you continue to see your chosen other through the soft-focus lens of love.

Were We Really a Match?

ONE WRITER PITS HIS MARRIAGE AGAINST THE HARD SCIENCE OF AN ONLINE DATING SITE

BY JOEL STEIN

During a low point of our relationship, my lovely wife, Cassandra, and I saw a couples therapist. I asked him to rate our marriage from 1 to 10. He gave us a 7. I think we would have gotten an 8 if Cassandra hadn't married the kind of guy who can understand emotions only through numbers.

Now, however, there's a scientific method to determine how our marriage ranks. The dating site eHarmony designed an algorithm to identify people who would make the happiest 25% of couples based on its research of thousands of marriages. At a psychology convention, the site presented findings showing that—contrary to academic beliefs—similar levels of traits like extroversion and intellect, not just general agreeableness, are the key to a successful marriage. If two people aren't enough alike in 29 categories, eHarmony won't match them and their marriage is going to suck. I had to know how we measured up.

OUR LOVE, TESTED

We drove to eHarmony's headquarters in one car, which I worried would needlessly drag out our breakup if we failed. Which I was pretty sure would happen. Our friends don't think we're well-matched. Cassandra is far cooler than I am and way less desperate for social validation. I, meanwhile, am much better at making my loved ones' negative traits sound like positives.

We walked into the eHarmony offices and sat down with Neil Clark Warren, the 82-year-old founder, who went to theological seminary and got a Ph.D. in psychology. His 55-year marriage seemed great, and his wife, who works a few offices down, seemed vivacious and devoted. Though I'm pretty sure Cassandra would be vivacious and devoted if I controlled a database of millions of single chicks.

Warren told us to sit on a couch and then said, "Do you intend to stay together for your lifetimes?" This seemed like an odd question to ask a married couple. Then we talked awhile, and I asked him if he was concerned. "It would be hard for me to say. It's clearly in the top half." This is the kind of muted encouragement one hears from a doctor after a cancer diagnosis.

Cassandra and I went to separate rooms to take a 110-question test. I finished in 15 minutes, partly because I kept hitting "Extremely" in response to the sex questions, causing the site to say, "Easy tiger!" and tell me to slow down. I was starting to think eHarmony had more in common with Cassandra than I did.

DEFYING THE DATA

After running three compatibility models, eHarmony vice president of matching Steve Carter told us that we were not a match. But on one test, we did score in the 74th percentile, just 1% shy of a match—and exactly the 7 the couples therapist gave us. What kept us from a higher score, Carter said, was that we both got a 0 for religious interest; eHarmony finds that atheists aren't often happily married. Also, Cassandra is 17% kinder than I am and has 37% more romantic passion. "You need to romance it up," said Carter. Then Cassandra said, "Actually, Joel is pretty good on that front and I could be better." For starters, she could give me a sexy pet nickname like the eHarmony questionnaire did.

On the drive home, we felt surprisingly fine. "When we met, I just felt the most myself with anyone I'd ever been with. I didn't think about compatibility," Cassandra had told me on the way to eHarmony. I had also not been thinking about compatibility. I had been thinking about how to get her naked. For two people not even thinking about marriage, we did all right.

What a Good Sex Life Looks Like

VARIETY HELPS, AND EVEN THE HAPPIEST OF COUPLES AREN'T PERFECTLY IN SYNC. FIND OUT WHAT ELSE RESEARCHERS KNOW ABOUT A SOLID SEXUAL FOUNDATION

BY HALLIE LEVINE

Ah, married sex. It's the topic of one-liner jokes and late-night talk shows. But the reality is that many of us are having more of it—and enjoying it more—than ever before. While more than 80% of people report being satisfied with their sex lives in the first six months of a relationship, about half—43% of men and 55% of women—reported still being content years later, according to a study published in 2016 in the *Journal of Sex Research* by the Kinsey Institute at Indiana University and Chapman University in Orange, Calif. "It's true that the first six months tend to be the most passionate and intense, and that that wears away over time," notes study author David Frederick, a professor of psychology at Chapman. "But our research shows there's plenty you can do to insert novelty and make it rewarding again." Here are eight things sexually satisfied couples do to keep a strong sex life going—often for decades.

The sex isn't every single day

Some days, when you're wiped from a day of work and an evening with the kids, the last thing you have the energy for

is doing the deed. The good news: studies prove you don't have to. When researchers surveyed more than 30,000 married or long-term monogamous couples, they found that while those who had more sex reported feeling happier, that benefit leveled off after once a week. "In other words, people who had sex four times a week had the same level of marital satisfaction as those who had sex just once a week," explains study author Amy Muise, an assistant professor in the department of psychology at York University in Toronto. "I think many couples feel pressured to have as much sex as possible, which can backfire: they feel so overwhelmed, they avoid it entirely. But ultimately it's the quality of the sex—and not the quantity—that truly counts."

It starts with housework (really)

Men, listen up: there's no better aphrodisiac than donning a pair of rubber gloves and doing the dishes. Couples who divvy up housework fairly equally report having more frequent and satisfying sex, according to a 2015 University of Alberta study published in the *Journal of Family Psychology*. This challenged previous research suggesting that when husbands perform traditional "women's work" (cooking, laundry), couples have less sex. "The argument was that men were emasculating themselves, but that didn't ring true to me after years of being a couples' therapist," says study author Matt Johnson, an assistant professor of family ecology at the university. "If you've got two people employed full-time outside the home, it makes sense that both partners doing their fair share prevents feelings of bitterness from building up, creating an environment much more conducive for sexual encounters to unfold."

There's intimacy in unsexy times

The more attentive a couple is to each other's emotional needs *outside* the bedroom, the higher their sexual desire for each other, per a University of Rochester study published in the *Journal of Personality and Social Psychology* in 2016. "This flies in the face of what's known as the 'intimacy-desire paradox'—the idea that when you get too close to

> **"Ultimately it's the quality of the sex—and not the quantity—that truly counts."**

a person, they stop feeling sexy and attractive to you because they're no longer strange and exotic," explains Harry Reis, a professor of psychology at Rochester. When Reis had 100 long-term couples keep a diary for six weeks to keep track of their sex drive, those who rated their partners most responsive to their needs also reported the highest libido. "When you feel valued, you also feel desirable, which in turn increases your own sex drive," says Reis. No idea where to start? Carve out 10 minutes a day to simply talk. "It's really important to just sit on the couch facing each other listening, without electronic devices on to distract you," advises Sheryl Brooks, a sex therapist at the Miraval Resort & Spa in Tucson, Ariz.

It includes three magic words

About three quarters of men and women with satisfying sex lives report saying "I love you" during their last sexual encounter, according to a Chapman University study published in 2016 in the *Journal of Sex Research*. "It seems to be the single most important communication strategy used among happy couples," says study author David Frederick. Here's why: it encourages you to bond psychologically with your partner, another important key for a happy sex life. The study also found that 1 in 3 women and 1 in 4 men who were sexually satisfied reported feeling more emotional closeness during sex now than at the start of their relationship.

It isn't strictly business as usual

Nothing makes for a more satisfying sex life than occasionally getting creative, according to the Chapman study. "If you're together for a decade, it can get pretty routine, which explains why the more acts of sexual variety couples engaged in, the more satisfied they were," says Frederick. "While almost half of all the couples in our study reported reading sex self-help books or magazine articles,

what set sexually satisfied couples apart was that they actually tried some of the ideas." While testing out a new position ranked on top, other strategies included taking a steamy bath together, giving each other massages, and talking about or acting out fantasies.

Date nights might just be playdates

It may really be true: mates who play together stay together. Couples who engage in adrenaline-raising, novel activities are happier, according to a study published in the *Journal of Personality and Social Psychology*. (Researchers strapped couples together with Velcro and had them crawl through an obstacle course—just the thing you want to be doing on Friday date night.) This may be because getting playful helps stave off boredom, which is the death of any relationship, notes Frederick, or it may be because these adventures ramp up your brain neurotransmitters, which are linked to sexual arousal. Don't worry: you don't have to book a tandem skydiving trip. "Any fun activity you used to do together, like biking or even just exploring new restaurants, can help bring that sexual spark back, as long as you do it with just one another," says Dion Metzger, a professor of psychiatry at the Morehouse School of Medicine.

Sometimes "yes" means "eh"

Truth is, couples are not always in sync: 80% of pairs report a desire discrepancy over the past month—meaning one wants sex but the other doesn't—according to research done by Muise. "The more someone was motivated to meet their partner's sexual needs, the stronger their overall sexual and relationship satisfaction," she explains. In other words, gearing yourself up for action when you would rather roll over and sleep brings benefits. "When people focused on the positives, like making their partner feel loved and desired, they actually got enjoyment out of it as well," Muise notes. Does that mean you should always cave in to your partner's requests for sex when you're not feeling it? No. "An important part of these communal relationships is both people are tuned in to each other's needs," emphasizes Muise. "That means also being understanding if your mate isn't in the mood."

Epic Displays of Affection

WHEN IT COMES TO EXPRESSING LOVE, SOME PEOPLE LIKE TO GO BIG. ARE THESE SPLASHY VALENTINES A SIGN OF DEEPER CONNECTION—OR JUST WANTON ACTS OF KOOKINESS?

BY DAN BOVA

Sixteen years ago, I asked my girlfriend to marry me. I'll spare you the lovey-dovey details of my proposal, but just know that there was some seriously lovey-dovey-ness going on. And since that day, I've made an effort to mark birthdays and anniversaries with fantastic gestures of affection to reflect the love in my heart.

Or so I thought.

Time has marched on, and some days when I'm scrolling through my phone while standing on the sidelines of my kids' soccer games (sorry, kids), I'll see a story pop into my Facebook feed like "Guy Spells Out 'I Love You' with 200 Kittens" or "Reality TV Star Buys Boyfriend a Watch That Costs More Than Your House." They're adorable stories tagged with a billion likes and hearts and surprised-face guys, and they also make me wonder whether maybe I'm not so great at this romance thing after all.

I've never once committed an EPDA, an Epic Public Display of Affection. I've never asked a life-changing question via Jumbotron. I've never jumped up and down on a couch à la Tom Cruise on daytime TV. I've never even really said "I love you" loudly in a crowded room.

Sure, things have worked out pretty well for us these past 16 years—two kids and a house that occasionally doesn't flood when it rains—but could I unintentionally be sending an "I don't care that much about you" message by never flashing my feelings across the sky?

Not likely, reassures therapist Terri Orbuch, also known as the Love Doctor. "There is this myth that a gesture like that must mean you really love someone," says Orbuch, a research professor at the University of Michigan's Institute for Social Research. "Some people believe, 'If I want to show that I am really in love and filled with happiness, I need to do something big to match my feelings.' " It's not really true.

A-list amour

While the average Joe is capable of over-the-top gestures, nobody has the ability to go super big like people with super big money. I'm talking, of course, about celebrities.

Case in point, Katy Perry. In 2010, the pop star bought an out-of-this-world gift for her then-fiancé, Russell Brand: a ticket on a Virgin Galactic flight to outer space. According to reports, the ticket cost $200,000 for a seat on a jet that will rocket passengers to the edge of space. (I find it pretty telling that she bought only one ticket.) Commercial flights on Virgin Galactic have yet to take off, but the couple's romance crashed and burned, ending in divorce after only 14 months of marriage.

Therein lies the rub. EPDAs reek of desperation, don't they? There's a certain "Hey, everyone, look at how oh-so-in-love we are!" quality about these headline-grabbing gifts. So are the givers just overcompensating? It's like that study a few years back that found that the couples who gush the most on Facebook about how amazing their relationship is are most likely to have meh relationships.

Someone should have told that to Richard Burton, who purchased a not-so-understated diamond for Elizabeth Taylor back in 1969. When a record-breaking 69.42-carat Harry Winston diamond went up for auction, Burton had a sneaking suspicion that Lizzie would like it. (Yes, he was that in tune with his lover's needs and wants.) Alas, Burton lost out to business tycoon Robert Kenmore, who bid more than a million bucks for the sparkler. But auctioneer hammer be damned, Burton wasn't taking no for an answer. He called Kenmore, haggled, begged and eventually won the diamond, which he dutifully gave to Taylor. All of that hard work paid off (for Liz, at least) when she hawked it for $5 million after they divorced.

Till death do us never part

In the case of India's Mughal emperor Shah Jahan, that need for recognition became one of the man-made wonders of the world. In 1631, Jahan's wife Mumtaz Mahal died during childbirth. Heartbroken, the shah tasked 20,000 workers with building her a marble and jewel-encrusted effigy. Twenty-two long years after work began, the place was finished. You might know it as the Taj Mahal. The chief mason who created it was thrilled at his accomplishment—for a minute, anyway. To ensure that its magnificence was never replicated, the shah commanded that the mason's right hand be chopped off.

For a slightly less epic (and definitely less bloody) gesture of postmortem amour, we turn to the baseball field. Simon and Garfunkel sang the question, "Where have you gone, Joe DiMaggio?" The answer: to the florist. When Joltin' Joe's ex-wife Marilyn Monroe died, he placed a standing order with a local flower shop for long-stem roses to be placed on her grave three times a week for 20 years.

I asked psychotherapist Michael McNulty, a certified Gottman relationship therapist at the Chicago Relationship Center, about these

Diamonds may be forever, but Liz Taylor and Richard Burton weren't: they married and divorced twice.

Eric Clapton wrote "Layla" for George Harrison's wife Pattie Boyd. They married, then split nine years later.

very sweet gestures to very dead women. "The thing that springs to mind is the line from the show *Fame* 'I'm gonna live forever,' " he says—the recipient may not be around to appreciate the gift, but the hope is that the memorial will ensure that the love they shared will live on in the memory of others.

Guilt can be at play as well, adds McNulty. "After the collapse of DiMaggio and Monroe's marriage, she fell under the negative influences of the Rat Pack and others. DiMaggio eventually reconnected with Marilyn and tried to support her recovery from addiction and psychological issues." The flowers, McNulty explains, may have been DiMaggio's attempt to make up for lingering regrets about how he treated her when she was alive.

Peace, lust and pajamas

If guilt drives lovers to excess, so can fear—fear that some jerk is going to swoop in and make a move on your love. An over-the-top gesture not only shows your sweetie that you mean business; it sends a clear message to the world: "Back off, here first!" There is certainly an element of human peacocking to EPDAs, says McNulty. "A grandiose gesture can be a way to state one's love to another and, at the same time, one-up the competition," he points out. "These gifts can be a way of saying, 'I love you the best. I'll do the most to keep you happy.' "

Planting a flag to say "This is mine" is typically thought to be a guy thing, but during the heyday of Brad Pitt and Angelina Jolie's marriage, it was Angie who did the planting. Literally. Jolie gave her hubby an olive tree (which seems rather ironic considering their recent not-so-nice separation). What is so epic about a tree? Well, it was a 200-year-old olive tree that cost $18,500 and was planted in the backyard of their $60 million estate in the South of France. Beats the hell out of the $18 tulips I bought for my wife and put in a $6 vase in the south of our kitchen.

Eric Clapton planted something a little less peaceful—an idea in the head of Pattie Boyd, his best friend George Harrison's wife, that she should leave the Beatle for him. Boyd turned down the guitarist's repeated pickup attempts, and, despondent, Clapton recorded the rock classic "Layla" to express his unrequited passion. Eventually, Boyd fell under Clapton's spell, split with Harrison and married her bluesman. Two months after getting hitched, the newlyweds had a party in Clapton's garden, the very same place where Harrison wrote "Here Comes the Sun." Harrison attended, which reportedly ended in an epic jam session. Perhaps love *is* all you need.

And also, pajamas.

The *Daily Mail* reported that one year for Christmas, David "Mr. Posh Spice" Beckham ordered two pairs of designer silk pajamas for his wife. At around $500 a pop, they're not cheap, but if you consider that the guy has a reported net worth of $350 million and change, that seems downright reasonable. Reminds me of the pair of J.Crew flannel pajamas that I bought my wife one year as a stocking stuffer. Out of all the gifts I've given her, I don't think anything has gotten more use, and given her more comfort, than those things. While I don't have nearly the amount of money, number of tattoos or visible abs that David Beckham has, it's nice to know that we shared the same thought: "I want my wife to be comfy."

So if you two exchange gifts that are more flannel than silk, take heart: it really is the thought that counts. As the Love Doctor, Terri Orbuch, reminds us, "It's the small things you do and say every day that predict happiness and longevity." Epic.

CHAPTER 2:

a Sacred

BOND

9 Signs Your Marriage Will Last

EVERYTHING FROM THE AGE WHEN YOU MARRIED TO WHETHER YOU SAY THANK YOU AFFECTS YOUR ODDS OF STAYING HAPPILY HITCHED. HERE ARE CLUES YOU TWO ARE IN IT FOR THE LONG HAUL

BY KATE ROCKWOOD

The odds that an American couple will celebrate their 20th wedding anniversary are roughly 50%, according to the National Center for Health Statistics. But that doesn't mean each of us is facing down the same coin toss. Psychologists and social scientists studying what makes one marriage last—happily!—while another dissolves into divorce have uncovered certain traits and habits that just may be predictors of lasting love.

1. You dated for a while (but had your own place)

Picking your paramour isn't the only pre-wedding move that may improve the longevity of your marriage. When Emory University researchers studied 3,000 married couples in the U.S., they found that couples who dated for three years or more before getting engaged were 39% less likely to divorce than those who saw each other for a year or less.

If you kept the keys to your own place during that extended getting-to-know-each-other period, you've got that going for you too. Women who didn't live with their partner before getting married had a 57% chance of celebrating their 20th anni-

versary, compared with 46% of women who cohabited. For men, the odds are similar: 60% of men who didn't live with their partner clocked 20 years of marriage, compared with 49% who shacked up before the big day.

2. You keep mmm-hmmms to a minimum

How do you respond when your spouse remarks on the unseasonably warm weather? Do you lift your face from your smartphone and suggest going on a walk? Or do you give a little "mmm-hmmm" without looking up? That stray comment may seem insignificant, but how you react can have a profound impact on how supported and known your partner feels, says Julie Gottman, a psychologist and renowned expert on marriage longevity who runs the Gottman Institute with her husband, John. "In long-lasting relationships, when one person makes a bid for connection or attention, the other person indicates in some way that they're paying attention and that they're interested," she says, "Turning toward the bidder shows interest and support, and that predicts longevity." In one study, the Gottmans tallied how couples reacted to a bid, then followed up six years later. Those who divorced had "turn-toward bids" just 33% of the time, while those still together hit 87%.

3. You amplify your partner's positive

Kudos for helping your spouse deal with setbacks like a job loss or medical scare. But how you respond to your mate's good news may actually make more of a difference in the long run. In the *Journal of Personality and Social Psychology*, psychological researcher Shelly Gable categorized couples' response styles along two dimensions: either passive or active (quiet or enthusiastic) and either constructive or destructive (supportive or demeaning). The study showed that the only difference between those couples who broke up or stayed together was an active-constructive response style. "When people get an active-constructive response to good news, they tend to savor it longer and have a better memory for it, even controlling for how important the news was on that day," says Gable. When you greet news of, say, your partner's promotion, with genuine interest—by asking questions, suggesting a celebratory dinner, listing the reasons she deserves it—it helps amplify her joy and creates an opportunity to bond. "How people responded to a partner's negative news was not predictive of a later breakup," says Gable. There's something to be said about wanting to stick with someone who makes your happy moments even happier.

4. You talk. Like, really talk

Unmarried couples, on average, chat for 50 minutes during an hour-long meal, according to a U.K. survey. But couples married for a decade talk for less than half the time. And those with young kids tend to talk to each other for just 10 minutes out of 60. Quantity isn't the only issue, says Terri Orbuch, a University of Michigan researcher who has studied 373 married couples for 30 years. "Many couples think they're communicating, but they're really doing household maintenance," she says. Sharing a funny anecdote or an interesting article with your spouse gets crowded out by the logistics of child care or lawn care or an aging parent. "That's why the second most-common divorce time is after 20 years of being together," Orbuch says. "Couples put communicating on the back burner until the kids are grown or the bills are paid off, but when you finally get there you don't know your partner." Long-lasting couples, she says, carve out times for conversations that mirror the early stages of a relationship: asking questions, sharing aspirations, and talking about anything but

How you respond to each other's good news may matter more than how you react to challenging times.

logistics. "It's not that you can't first talk about work or kids or your mother who's in the hospital," she says. "But for a long-lasting marriage, you also need to talk about other things for at least 10 minutes at least a few times a week."

5. *You had warm feet on your wedding day*

Men tend to experience "cold feet," or premarital doubts, more often than women, according to researchers at UCLA, but it's whether women get them that is predictive of a brief marriage. In the study, which was published in the *Journal of Family Psychology*, women who had reported having cold feet before they got hitched were more than twice as likely to be divorced four years later as brides who didn't experience those last-minute doubts.

Honeymoons might also be a harbinger of a successful marriage. Emory University researchers found that people who got away post-wedding were 41% less likely to split than those who stayed put. One surprising wedding factor that doesn't create long-lasting unions: a flashy ceremony. In fact, lovebirds who shelled out more than $20,000 to tie the knot were 46% more likely to part ways. According to lead researcher Andrew Francis-Tan, an economics professor at Emory University, overspending may lead to debt stress, which can strain a marriage.

6. *You fight fair*

Whether you're miserable or merry in your marriage has less to do with how often you have conflict and more to do with how you handle it. Contempt is the No. 1 predictor of divorce, says Gottman. "When you have contempt, you're fighting from a position of superiority, sneering in disgust," she says. Think name-calling, eye-rolling or mocking with sarcasm. It's nearly impossible to resolve something once superiority and disgust slip into the frame.

But contempt isn't the only fighting style that can signal the death knell of a marriage: In 40 years of studying marriage, the Gottmans have developed a system of categorizing couples into masters (those in thriving marriages) and disasters (those in failed or foundering unions), and they identify three other "horsemen of the apocalypse" besides contempt that spell trouble for a union: defensiveness (like always claiming you're a victim), criticism (pinning a problem on your partner's flawed personality) and stonewalling (shutting down or walking out).

While those problematic fighting styles might seem easy enough to spot—at least once the heated moment has passed—there's a more subtle SOS the body sends out in a distressed marriage. In following thousands of couples longitudinally, the Gottmans brought them into the lab and used electrodes to measure their physiological responses. "What we saw is that when disasters were having a conflict discussion, their bodies went into fight-or-flight mode," says Gottman. Heart rates jumped to more than 100 beats per minute, blood flow quickened, sweat glands kicked into overdrive—even if the tenor of the conflict seemed tame. "During that kind of physiological flooding, there's more blood moving from the frontal lobe to the modal cortex, as your body prepares to fight or flee, and that causes tunnel vision and tunnel hearing," she says. Forget parsing the nuance of a partner's argument—in this state, people are more likely to get aggressive and attack. And the Gottmans found that the more physiologically active the couples were in the lab, the quicker their relationships deteriorated over time.

Few people can recognize when their heart rate quickens, but there might be another cue—say, a sweaty back—that signals adrenaline is in overdrive. And couples can calm that fight-or-flight response simply by taking a break. "When people who are starting to get flooded separate for 30 minutes to self-soothe, with reading or taking a walk or yoga, the conversation is much more successful," says Gottman. The trick is to set a time to reconvene, so neither person feels abandoned, and to not spend the break ruminating on the conflict itself.

The most successful marriages have a ratio of five positive feelings and actions to every one that's negative.

7. You've got demographics on your side

Marital longevity is more likely if you've been dealt a certain set of factors and circumstances. A college education is one: 78% of women with a B.A. under their belt who married for the first time could expect their marriage to last 20 years, according to researchers at the National Center for Health Statistics. For women without a degree, that figure slumps to 40%. For men, the impact of education on marriage isn't quite as pronounced, but it's still present: 65% of graduates could expect to hit two decades of marriage, compared with 50% for those with a high school diploma or less.

Age is another factor that increases your odds for marital success, but the relationship is not as linear as many think: while couples who tie the knot in their teens are significantly more likely to divorce than those who wed in their 20s, the rate of divorce rises once people hit their mid-30s, according to an analysis by the Institute for Family Studies. In fact, the odds of divorce for a first-time marriage increase by 5% per year, starting at the age of 32.

8. You both carve out "me time"

When Orbuch crunched data on the couples she has followed for 30 years, she found that nearly twice as many people pointed to a lack of personal time making them unhappy as a lackluster sex life. Couples who are constantly together often give up hobbies or interests that only one half loves (antiquing, anyone?). But that's not the only reason nonstop togetherness might lead to marital trouble. "When people have their own friends and hobbies, they're able to define themselves beyond their relationship, and that makes them happier," says Orbuch. It also means that when you two come back together, you have more to talk about and share. "It makes them less bored," she says. And Orbuch's study, which was published in *Psychological Science*, shows that couples who report boredom in the seventh year of marriage were significantly less likely to be satisfied with their relationship by the 16th year.

9. You cultivate a culture of mutual appreciation

While "disasters" tend to be on the lookout for small grievances and mistakes, marriage "masters" have their antennae tuned for all the things they can be grateful for, says Gottman. "Our research shows that a rich climate of appreciation is a big predictor of a long-lasting, healthy relationship," she says. "People don't think their partner really needs it or already knows it, so they stop saying what they appreciate and start to take the person for granted."

Sharing frequent appreciation—for making the coffee this morning, for calling to check in, for reorganizing the garage—doesn't only make your partner feel recognized; it encourages other feel-good interactions. The Gottmans' research shows that the most successful, long-lasting marriages have a ratio of five positive feelings and actions for every one that's negative. (Think of appreciative comments as tipping the ratio in your favor.)

Appreciation also plays a central role in affirmation, along with showering your partner with small acts or love and kindness. And in Orbuch's Early Marriage Project, she found that regular affirmation predicts that a couple is almost twice as likely to stay together.

Men have an even greater need for affirmation than women, Orbuch's data suggest. Those who didn't feel affirmed by their wives were twice as likely to divorce as those who did. The same didn't hold for the other gender. "We've been taught as women that it's OK to give affirmations to our friends, family, coworkers, even other women on the sidewalk," says Orbuch, "so we have a broader network of affirmations." Men, on the other hand, tend to be more tight-lipped beyond the marriage, and so they feel a deeper need for kindness and appreciation at home.

The Health Perks of Saying "I Do"

GET HITCHED, AND YOU'RE IN FOR MORE THAN LOVE AND COMPANIONSHIP. BETTER HEALTH AND A LONGER LIFE ARE PART OF THE DEAL—IF YOU TWO ARE HAPPY

BY LORI OLIWENSTEIN

Never mind the popular palaver about a good marriage as a source of bliss for the couple, security for the kids and stability for society. Plenty of spouses—at least after the first year—come to see it as a lot of work. And why shouldn't they? Pair up any two people with often clashing needs; add kids, bills, career, housework and the fact that someone—he knows who he is—can't pull himself away from the TV during college-basketball season; and there are bound to be problems. Marriage is criticized as a source of stress (and it is), conflict (that too) and endless crises that need to be resolved (guilty there as well).

But it's also something more. Decades of data collection have shown that marriage, for all its challenges, is like a health-insurance policy, especially if the union is a strong one. A 2006 paper that tracked mortality over an eight-year period found that people who never married were 58% likelier to die during that time than married folks were.

And no wonder. Marriage means no more drinking at singles' bars until closing, no more eating uncooked ramen noodles out of the bag and calling it a meal. According to a 2004 report from the Centers for Disease Control and Prevention (CDC), married people are less likely to smoke or drink heavily than people who are single, divorced or widowed. These sorts of lifestyle choices are associated with lower rates of cardiovascular disease, cancer and respiratory diseases.

Partners in wellness

That's not all. A 2015 study out of the University of Missouri found that marriage helps older adults sleep longer and better than those who drift off without a partner by their side. And while you may sometimes gripe that your spouse is driving you nuts, just the opposite is generally true. Married people have lower rates of all types of mental illnesses. They're also less likely to commit suicide.

The health benefits are largely consistent across age, race, education and income groups, and although researchers have not conducted equally exhaustive studies of gay couples, benefits probably flow to them too.

Some of the reasons for this are obvious. Smoking and drinking naturally decline if you've got a concerned spouse at your side flashing you a don't-you-dare look when you reach for a cigarette or a third glass of wine. Depression, anxiety and other emotional ills are less likely to go unnoticed when there is someone at home who's mindful of your moods. But there are other, less self-evident reasons—things that experts are only now beginning to appreciate fully.

Marriage on the brain

Much of what makes marriage so healthy for us takes place within our own bodies, entirely without our knowledge. A lot of those benefits come down to stress—or, specifically, the management of it. Stress puts into motion a biological cascade involving hormones, glands and neural circuits, all activating one another in a complex feedback loop.

When you are stuck in traffic or overwhelmed at work or worn down by the kids, the hypothalamus—a structure buried deep in the midbrain—tells your adrenal gland to pump out a supply of the stress hormone cortisol. Cortisol, in turn, instructs your body to stop worrying about its basic metabolic needs and instead "do the things you need to do to save yourself from whatever created the stress," says University of Virginia neuroscientist James Coan.

That's great if you're fleeing a bear, since to save yourself you need to boost your heart rate and respiration, tense your muscles, and generally crank up your body's alertness level. But such an energy-intensive system is designed to be used only in brief bursts; you either escape that bear or you get eaten by it, but either way the crisis ends. The daily stresses of modern life, on the other hand, can throw our bodies into that kind of acute emergency mode and keep us there. That takes a toll through high blood pressure, tension headaches and a lot of gnawed pencils. "If you're chronically releasing stress hormones,

your body starts to fall apart," says Coan. "Ultimately, you're going to live less long—and you're going to be miserable."

A strong marriage protects you; a bad marriage can harm you

Being married somehow helps the body circumvent this mess, either by hushing the hypothalamus or reducing cortisol production. Coan and his colleagues conducted an experiment in which married women underwent brain scans using functional magnetic resonance imaging. During the scans, the women were told they were going to receive a painful electric shock. The researchers then watched to see how the subjects' brains responded to the threat and found that among happily married women, hypothalamus activity declined sharply if husbands held their wives' hands during the experiment. Women who reported being less satisfied with their marriage—and women whose hands were held by strangers—got little such relief. "The effect was pretty profound," says Coan. "It was much stronger than we thought it would be."

If you are happily married, your spouse may function as a painkiller, according to one brain study.

He also found that spousal hand holding had an effect in a different part of the brain: the right anterior insula, which responds to the threat of pain by calling your attention to the part of your body that's in danger, increasing the amount of discomfort you ultimately feel. In Coan's study, the right anterior insula of happily married women stayed relatively quiet while they received news of the shocks.

"This suggests," he says, "that your spouse may function as an analgesic."

Men benefit more than women

All of this is especially good news for men. A study published in 2008 in the journal *Health Psychology* showed that while married men get relief from their workday barrage of stress hormones when they come home after a particularly busy day at the office, working women are able to de-stress in the same way only if they describe their marriage as a happy one.

There may be a simple explanation for this. "I'm speculating," says Rena Repetti, a professor of psychology at the University of California, Los Angeles, and one of the authors of the study, "but it may just be that some of these women are coming home and facing dinner prep and assisting the kids with homework, and they're not getting the help that the more maritally satisfied women are getting."

The full explanation for this gender gap, however, is undoubtedly more complicated. Long-term data from an Israeli study, for example, indicates that the life-lengthening powers of marriage have increased over time—but again, mostly for men. Over nearly two decades, married men widened the already significant difference in cancer-death incidence between themselves and unmarried men by 25%; married women, on the other hand, gained absolutely zero ground over their unmarried peers.

Why this subtle somatic sexism? "This is a gross generalization, but women are really the mental- and physical-health housekeepers for a marriage," points out psychologist Janice Kiecolt-Glaser of the Ohio State University College of Medicine. "They are often

the ones who prod men to go to a doctor or to eat more healthily."

In fact, a 2016 study of heterosexual couples over 50 found that happily married men, particularly ones with well-educated wives, were more likely than single men to have gotten a colonoscopy in the previous five years. Interestingly, the same wasn't true of women: married women were no more likely than single women to have had this colon cancer screening test, and their partners' education level didn't make a difference.

When things turn bad

For all its benefits, marriage is not a gift certificate for good health. For one thing, it's fattening. A 2016 look at 20 years of data by Jay Teachman from Western Washington University found that single or divorced people, no matter their gender, are thinner than those who are cohabiting. And a CDC study of health and marriage similarly determined that married people, while least likely to be physically inactive, are most likely to be overweight or obese.

Married guys, in particular, seem to pack on the pounds after they say their vows. They are nearly 20% more likely to be overweight or obese than are men who have never married—perhaps because they simply have someone to sit down to dinner with each night.

Data also shows that the stress of a bad marriage can undo much of the good that comes with a happy one. A 2014 analysis of 126 articles on health and marriage published over the past half-century found that the better your marriage is, the lower your risk of mortality at any point in time compared with those of your less-happily-married friends.

In a series of studies, Kiecolt-Glaser and her husband, immunologist Ronald Glaser, also of the Ohio State University College of Medicine, found that "negative marital interactions," such as arguments, name-calling and nonverbal cues like eye rolling lead to increases in cortisol and decreases in immune function and even wound-healing. Though the effects were observed in both sexes, they were particularly strong in women.

Data shows the stress of a bad marriage can undo much of the good that comes with a happy one.

The eye-rolling studies go even deeper than that, with related research conducted by John Gottman of the Gottman Institute in Seattle revealing just how sensitive spouses are to such nonverbal signs of disdain or dismissal. Coan, who has collaborated with Gottman, says, "How often someone rolls their eyes at you can predict how often you need to go to the doctor."

A broken heart just may be real

And when the protective bonds of marriage break, watch out. Those supposedly apocryphal tales of spouses who die within days of each other have more than a little truth to them. A 2007 British study found that at any given moment, a bereaved spouse has a greater risk of death from just about any cause (except, oddly, lung cancer) than a still-married person. "Over time," says Coan, "your brain becomes used to the other person as part of your emotional-regulation strategy. You take that person away, and you become what we dryly call dysregulated—weepy, mournful, staying up half the night. This can come from death, divorce, even a long business trip. When those bonds break, it can cause a lot of pain and emotional suffering."

Taking the long view

Certainly not all suddenly single spouses are fated to languish this way—no more than others who never pair off are destined for a shortened life filled with illness and stress. Humans are socially resourceful creatures who build and rebuild networks of relationships, getting the attention, hand holding and even scolding they need in a lot of different ways.

Still, it's hard to argue with an institution that keeps a companion and caretaker constantly nearby, even if now and again—when a wet towel has once again been dropped on the bedroom floor or a tube of toothpaste has been squeezed all wrong—we lose sight of that happy fact.

10 Ways to Make Your Marriage Divorce-Proof

FOR STARTERS, NO PUBLIC SQUAWKING AT EACH OTHER. READ ON FOR MORE SMART (AND FUNNY) RELATIONSHIP DO'S FROM HAPPILY WED COMEDIANS

BY SAMANTHA BEE AND JASON JONES

We have been hitched for 15 years now [that's us on the facing page], and until recently our number-one piece of advice would have been: Don't write about how to make your marriage divorce-proof. It's hubris! But we like to take risks (that's piece of advice number two), so we knocked on wood, threw salt over our shoulders, and forged ahead with all the unstoppable energy that a couple with three kids can muster. (Eating a pile of old Halloween candy helped too.) Ultimately, we came up with this list of marriage rules and reminders—all of which, we hope, are cheaper and more fun than therapy.

1. Realize that if you can agree on what constitutes a clean room, you can agree on anything

If you are the kind of person who wants the vacuum tracks on the living-room carpet to last all week (as in, Jason), you need to understand that your spouse is physically unable to hover three inches off the floor when traveling from point A to point B. You may have to shoulder the burden of raking the shag rug twice a day yourself. Conversely, if you are the type of person who "gets around" to wiping up a raw-chicken-juice spill on the counter (for example, Sam), you should know that if you want to live with other humans, you need to surpass the hygiene standards of, say, the average fraternity-house bathroom. Fortunately, if you can compromise on the red-hot-button subject of cleanliness, your marriage is unlikely to be thrown off course by comparatively less volatile topics, like politics, religion and money.

2. If you're irritated by your partner, imagine him as a small child

We know! You totally don't want to try this! It sounds awful! (And maybe even not that much of a stretch.) But trust us—this is an amazing way to see him from a fresh angle. Here's what to do: While your partner is puttering around and looking idle, imagine him at age 5. Awww. Isn't he adorable? And so smart! It's easy to forget how appealing your spouse is when you are looking at him through a prism of all the chores that he has yet to accomplish (fixing the garage-door opener, booking the tree-removal service … we could go on).

3. No fisticuffs in public

Take this example: We were at a picnic with a group of friends when the wife in one of the couples present casually announced that she had bought their family a house. In another country. Without consulting the husband. He turned about 14 shades of red, and they began fighting at the top of their lungs. Cut to everyone else with their heads down, forensically examining their egg-salad sandwiches as though they contained the secrets of the human genome. You do not want to be That Couple Who Ruined the Otherwise Delightful Picnic.

4. Marry someone with a backbone who appreciates that you possess one of your own

That said, try to have bendy backbones if possible. Don't attempt to win every argument and get your way all the time. Who could bear all that responsibility, anyway? Repeat this spouse-mollifying phrase after us: "Yes, honey, I will see the *Transformers* sequel on one of our precious and rare date nights. But on our next excursion, I get to choose a period piece featuring people in bonnets who churn their own butter."

5. Procrastinate

Yes, we know things need to be done, but seriously. Put your phone away and stop worrying about the broken garage-door opener. Have dessert in lieu of dinner. Watch old John Hughes movies. Hold hands. There, aren't they smoother than how you remembered them?

6. Have sex with each other

And if you can't have sex with each other for some reason, let your spouse know you are thinking about having sex with him and that you are looking forward to the next time you are both available for sex. Like, in 2018. Try sending a "sext"; apparently it's all the rage.

7. Accept that everybody needs some alone time

Sometimes your spouse needs to go to the bathroom for 45 minutes. Look, he's not going to the bathroom the whole time; he's trying to get away from you. And that's OK. Maybe you're being annoying. Sometimes you can be kind of annoying, you know.

8. If you have to fight, walk and fight

In our experience, arguments stem more from being cooped up together in tight quarters than from the issue at hand. Plus, getting fresh air is good for you, and it will give you more energy for No. 6. (Hey, everyone knows that makeup No. 6 is the best kind.)

9. Let your spouse in on 90% of your day-to-day routine

Save the other 10% for your bathroom time. Sam, for example, will never allow Jason to see her lurching to put on a pair of pantyhose, and he never wishes for her to see him struggling to shave the back of his neck. It's those small things that keep the mystery alive.

10. When you buy gifts for each other, give them at least a full minute of thought

Sam's mother once gave her partner a giant meat grinder for Christmas so that he (an extremely reluctant cook) could make her tastier hamburgers. In our opinion, gifts that require someone to perform a household task don't count as gifts. A present should convey the message "I love you, but most of all, I get you." (Yes, that's a tough sentiment to express with a big-box-store gift card. Ahem.) Like playing chess or figuring out Facebook privacy settings, delighting a longtime spouse is a genuine challenge—which (duh) is what makes it worth the effort.

Once a Cheat, Always a Cheat?

AFFAIRS OPERATE ON SEX, LUST AND BETRAYAL AND, IN THE END, DOOM THE MARRIAGE—RIGHT? IT'S NOT SO SIMPLE: THE TRUTH ABOUT WHO STRAYS AND WHAT INFIDELITY MEANS IS MORE COMPLICATED

BY JACQUELINE ANDRIAKOS

We think of the clichés: the long-married banker who shacks up with his young associate on a business trip. Or the bored suburban mom who takes off with her tennis instructor. Yet researchers are learning that there is no profile of a cheater, just as there is no blueprint for infidelity. In truth, the drivers of cheating—not to mention the consequences of it—vary greatly, and they're often unpredictable, says Esther Perel, a psychotherapist and relationship counselor and author of *Mating in Captivity: Unlocking Erotic Intelligence*. "What we do know is every affair will redefine a marriage, for worse or for better."

Myth #1: Infidelity is a sign of an unhappy marriage

Women are indeed more likely than men to cheat due to lack of gratification or happiness in their marriage, but the male motivation tends to be different. "Men are simply more opportunistic," says Barry Kuhle, an assistant professor of psychology at the University of Scranton. "If the opportunity to cheat presents itself, males are more likely to engage, even if they are perfectly

content with their partner." In fact, according to a study in the journal *Sex Roles*, 56% of men said they were happy in their marriages, despite having extramarital affairs.

In general, people tend to stray because they feel discontented with themselves, not with their partner, adds psychotherapist and marriage counselor Rachel Sussman. "You might have a strong marriage, but maybe your husband or wife grapples with low self-esteem, is having qualms about getting older," she says. "It's frequently an internal psychological trouble taking place that has nothing to do directly with the relationship."

Myth #2: Cheating is all about sex

Both sexual and emotional betrayals sting, as HBO's series *Divorce* nails when Thomas Haden Church's and Sarah Jessica Parker's characters bicker in couples therapy over whether his emotional dalliance counts as an affair and whether it can be considered nearly as evil as her sex-driven sideshow. Let's face it: in this era of Facebook-friendship-turned-flirtation and late-night sexting, the act of intercourse is not even required for things to cross a line. "There is no agreement on a definition of infidelity, not even in the research," Perel says. What's clear, though, is that "you don't need to have actual physical contact to have some sort of sexual, intimate experience." Psychiatrist Scott Haltzman, author of *The Secrets of Surviving Infidelity*, agrees: "I think couples need better understandings of emotional affairs, because if you don't understand what emotional infidelity is, you can't prevent it, and you end up getting into arguments with your spouse about whether you did or didn't have an affair."

What's more, the physical act often isn't what hurts the other spouse the most, explains Kuhle, who has researched the role of jealousy in romantic relationships. Men are more likely to focus on the sexual aspects of their partner's infidelity, his studies have suggested, while women are more likely to be hung up on the emotional implications of a tryst. "A woman who has been cheated on likely isn't interrogating about the sex like a male might," Kuhle explains. "They're questioning the depths of the relationship: How many times did you lie to me? Have our kids ever met this woman? Are you in love with her?"

Myth #3: Powerful men stray the most

Sussman has a girlfriend who's married to a big-shot CEO. "One of our mutual friends said to me, 'She's lucky he doesn't cheat on her.' I remember thinking, What kind of a comment is that?" Sussman recalls. "But that's how a lot of people think, that men, money and power equals a wandering eye." She says that while the headline-grabbing affairs we hear about often star a high-profile man (Bill Clinton, Tiger Woods, Arnold Schwarzenegger), status is only one of any number of affair triggers. Interestingly, a recent study published in the *American Sociological Review* found that men with breadwinner wives cheat three times as much as women who are economically dependent on their husbands.

Infidelity, it turns out, is an equal-opportunity temptation. Men tend to get the bad rap for being roamers, yet a 2011 survey from Indiana University showed that the numbers of men and women who stray are nearly neck and neck, with the percentages for both sexes hovering just above and below 20%, respectively. And they're not your central-casting version of womanizers and femme fatales: "The majority of men and women who are unfaithful are not chronic philanderers or narcissists," Perel says. "They are your average people who have been faithful for years. They come to me with this conflict between their values and their behavior, and they don't know how they got there."

Myth #4: If it happened once, it'll happen again

The serial cheater exists, for sure, but it's a niche category of adulterers, according to Haltzman. "When people say 'Once a cheater, always a cheater,' they're talking about a

very specific type of infidelity that's far less common, where someone is actively seeking an extramarital affair." Think the married woman on a dating site behind closed doors, or a man who takes off his wedding ring at the bar. A recent study published in the *Archives of Sexual Behavior* surveyed more than 700 men and women in long-term relationships, and among those who cheated on former partners, 70% said they had not cheated on their current significant other.

Myth #5: People know when they are playing with fire

"We don't always understand our natures or comprehend romantic traps that might be in front of us," Haltzman says. Take flirtation, for example: studies show that women are typically better at understanding body language than men, as well as reading tone in conversation. "You could say to a guy, 'It's so obvious that that person is flirting with you,' but from a psychological point of view, he truly may not have been able to recognize that on a conscious level," he explains.

While you can't completely affair-proof a marriage, there is something you can do to prevent a side friendship from turning romantic: recognize it as a potential threat to your marriage, says Haltzman. "Flirting feels good, which is why boundaries are important. If you allow an emotional affair to grow long enough and without sufficient obstacles, it will almost invariably lead to a sexual affair."

Biology may actually help us stay faithful: Harvard anthropological research suggests that marriage in and of itself dampens men's cravings for sexual exploration. Men experience a dip in testosterone after tying the knot, a possible evolutionary mechanism to reduce their drive to mate. "So you might expect men's inclination to cheat to go down after that milestone," Kuhle says, "but there really needs to be more research about that."

Myth #6: An affair always destroys a couple's marriage

While many marriages do break up once a partner learns the other has been unfaithful, a surprisingly high percent don't (up to 80% of couples stay together). Many variables affect a pair's chances of pulling through, including whether the third party is someone both spouses know, how long the affair lasted, whether it did become sexual, and whether the person hurt by the infidelity is willing to forgive and move on.

Healing requires asking some probing questions to help identify the meaning and the motive of the affair (Why did it happen? Can and will you end it? Do you want to change?), Sussman says—while not pressing for the R-rated details.

Forgiveness often comes in baby steps. "The person asking for a second chance needs to really see the full picture of what he or she is asking for forgiveness for," Haltzman says. This requires listening closely: Is it the pain that you lied to him? That you gave yourself emotionally to someone else? After that, the partner who committed the infidelity needs to lay out what he or she will do differently to make it up to their mate. "It's an involved process," he adds, "and therapy helps many couples follow the necessary steps."

And in fact, many couples who stay and work hard to get past the affair together come out on the other side stronger than before. This is partly because infidelity spurs a more open dialogue, Perel notes. "In the aftermath of an affair, people finally start to talk about what their unmet needs are; where they have gone stale," she says. "Suddenly there is something to fight for."

The (Real) Key to a Joyful Union

IT ISN'T SEX (THOUGH IT MAY HELP ON THAT FRONT). IT ISN'T GRATITUDE, EITHER. HERE'S WHY GOOD OLD-FASHIONED COMPASSION IS WHAT A MARRIAGE NEEDS MOST

BY CAMILLE NOE PAGÁN

Your spouse forgot his credit card at a restaurant again. Sure, you could roll your eyes or snap, "When are you going to get more organized?" But if you instead say, "I'm sorry, can I help?" you will improve his day and your own in the process.

No doubt you've heard about the perks of optimism and gratitude. Think of compassion—the feeling of concern and/or sympathy for another's misfortune, along with a desire to lend a hand—as their equally gifted but less hyped sister. "It's the key to happiness and well-being," says Thupten Jinpa, a former Buddhist monk who helped develop a landmark course in compassion training at Stanford School of Medicine. Indeed, a growing body of research shows that compassion reduces anxiety, depression and stress and may boost immunity, along with longevity.

But that's not all: a new study of 1,500 married Americans in the journal *Family Relations* found that when spouses were humble and compassionate toward each other, they were less stressed and more satisfied in their relationships."Other research has shown that learning to communicate well doesn't actually improve romantic relationships the way you might expect," says study author Jonathan Olson, an associate professor of public health and health

psychology at Bastyr University, a nonprofit institution of science-based natural medicine. "But our study found that focusing on certain traits that fall under the umbrella of communication—that is, humility and compassion—does make marriages happier." That may be because compassion, in particular, smoothes out the inevitable rough spots in a relationship: "Being able to see the other person's perspective and want to help makes it easier to move past conflict," explains Olson.

Hardwired for happiness

We're born with the instinct to be nice. Even babies and toddlers have the capacity for kindness. One study in the journal *PLOS One* found that kids under the age of 2 were happier when they gave treats to another person than when they received treats themselves. Doing for others actually gives you a veritable high. Donating money lights up the brain's pleasure centers, which are typically activated by things like food and sex, according to a study in the *Proceedings of the National Academy of Sciences*. Some experts believe that there's an evolutionary explanation: by lending a hand, we up the odds that our species will survive, so our bodies prime us for the behavior by making helping feel good.

Simply witnessing an act of compassion triggers feelings of admiration, warmth and love, per a study in the *Journal of Positive Psychology* (which may be why we click on stories about people who donate a kidney to a stranger). Compassion also curbs the natural (and anxiety-provoking) tendency to navel-gaze. "When you're responding to someone else's needs, your focus is off yourself," explains Jinpa, author of *A Fearless Heart*. That can quiet self-critical thought patterns ("Do I do enough for my family?" "Do I look old for my age?"), helping you feel better overall.

The kindness cure

If compassion can make your home happier, why don't we all practice it more often? The very fact that your partner is a capable adult may dampen your desire to jump to his or her aid, says Stan Tatkin, a psychotherapist and assistant clinical professor at the David Geffen School of Medicine at UCLA. "You may be

Simply witnessing an act of compassion triggers feelings of admiration, warmth and love.

compassionate to your kids, for example, because they may seem more helpless and therefore are easier to empathize with."

You might also be afraid that being that understanding when your mate messes up puts you in a bad position, but nothing could be further from the truth. "When you show your partner compassion, they're more likely to do the same for you. In a way, you're really helping yourself as well as your spouse, which improves your overall relationship," points out KC Haydon, an assistant professor of psychology and education at Mount Holyoke College.

Then there's the stress factor. Pressing emotions like worry can crowd out our generous nature. "With life being as hectic as it is, it's all too easy to fall into the mind-set that you don't have time to go out of your way for anyone else—even your own partner," says Stefanie Ziev, a life coach in New York. "Yet compassion isn't necessarily something big or dramatic. In many cases, it's little actions or thoughts." It can be as simple as saying, "Listen, I'll pack the kids' lunches for you today" or "Hey, I know you're stressed about the bills, but you're doing a great job."

As with many things in life, the more you practice, the more natural it becomes. Here are a few strategies for starting this powerful habit.

1. Set a daily intention

For example, write "I intend to bring joy to my husband/wife today" on a Post-it and stick it on the back of your smartphone (or make it your wallpaper). This can set the tone for your entire day and may just change the outcomes of all your interactions, not just with your mate. "People tend to reflect the emotions others are projecting," says Ziev.

2. Be mindful

The ability to focus on the present promotes empathy by instilling a sense of calm. To cul-

3 WAYS TO SHOW YOURSELF THE LOVE

Don't forget to be nice to you. "About 80% of people are more compassionate to others than they are to themselves," says Kristin Neff, an associate professor of human development and culture at the University of Texas. "There's a misconception that self-compassion is selfish, but being kind to yourself puts you in a happier, more pleasant mind-set, and that allows you to have better relationships with others."

1. CHECK THAT DOWNER VOICE IN YOUR HEAD

Instead of the punitive "OMG, I'm late again because my life is such a mess!" try "I deserve credit for getting my family out the door every morning." Says Neff, "I tell my students to talk to themselves the way they would talk to a friend."

2. ADMIT WHEN THINGS STINK

Say you've racked up a lot of debt, and it's weighing on you and your partner. Or you're trying to lose weight and can't, but a good friend is having no trouble shedding pounds. "Rather than sugarcoating the situation, acknowledge that it's painful, it's part of life, and it will pass," says Jean Fain, author of *The Self-Compassion Diet*. "Being honest about your feelings invites you to be kinder to yourself."

3. PUT YOUR HAND ON YOUR HEART

No, really. "People respond deeply to touch, even from themselves," says Neff. "This can send a soothing message from your body to your mind and put you in a compassionate state."

tivate more mindfulness in daily life, "take a few minutes to meditate while sitting in a chair or walking around the neighborhood," advises Jean Fain, a psychotherapist and instructor at Harvard Medical School. "Start by wishing good for yourself. Repeat a phrase such as 'May I be safe, may I be happy, may I live with ease' 5 to 10 times. Then wish the same for your friends and family."

3. Move more

Repetitive exercise, like running, also encourages you to stay more present. In fact, aerobic exercise is more effective at cultivating mindfulness than relaxation training, found a 2014 study in *Mental Health and Physical Activity*. Researchers suspect this is because physical activity activates brain regions that control attention.

4. Hit the pause button

If your other half says something unkind in the middle of a fight, don't snap back. Instead, take a deep breath. "That kind of behavior is almost always a distress signal that means the partner needs something they're not getting," says Haydon (who has watched thousands of hours of couples arguing). After pausing, try saying, "We're having a disconnect here, and it seems like I'm not understanding what you mean. Can you try to explain it to me?" That tiny gesture can not only defuse the tension, but also lead to a positive shift—helping the two of you get on the same page.

5. Use your (positive) imagination

It's human nature to judge others. But when your wife leaves the milk out (again), is it possible she was rushing to get the kids out the door on time? If your husband doesn't come on to you at night, could it be he's just dead tired? "Compassion requires you to give people the benefit of the doubt," notes Jinpa. That doesn't mean you should become everyone's favorite doormat, but do your best to let unkind asides and disappointing actions go. And if you screw up, extend yourself the benefit of the doubt too—you'll do better next time. After all, you deserve to get as much tenderness as you give.

BARACK +

MICHELLE OBAMA

Because if *they* have time to keep the spark alive, we all do. Michelle posted this about Barack on Instagram in August 2016: “55 years young and that smile still gets me every single day.”

Hall of Fame Couples

SEVEN EXTRAORDINARY PAIRS, POWERFUL FOR THEIR TOGETHERNESS

PAUL NEWMAN +

JOANNE WOODWARD

The Oscar winner once quipped about staying faithful to Woodward, with whom he had three daughters, "Why go out for hamburger when you can get steak at home?"

ELLEN DEGENERES +
PORTIA DE ROSSI

DeGeneres told *People* in 2016 that the secret to her happy marriage to her "best friend," de Rossi, is gratitude. "Portia and I constantly say to each other, 'We are so lucky.' "

TIM MCGRAW + FAITH HILL

The country music stars have been honest about the grit it takes to sustain a 20-year marriage: McGraw recently credited his wife and three daughters with inspiring him to stop partying. This spring, the pair kick off a joint tour.

JOHN LENNON + YOKO ONO

From their honeymoon Bed-In for Peace to their haunting final album—released just weeks before Lennon was murdered outside their New York apartment building—John and Yoko reminded the world that two voices are more powerful than one.

The Finals

STEPHEN + AYESHA CURRY

The Golden State Warriors star and his wife, who have two daughters, are all about blending work and family. Steph stole hearts bringing Riley, now 4, to work (read: press conferences). And Ayesha shares family recipes in her cookbooks.

PRINCE WILLIAM + PRINCESS KATE

Will and Kate's Westminster Abbey wedding may have been steeped in tradition, but their relationship is refreshingly modern, with date nights and the hands-on parenting of young George and Charlotte.

CHAPTER 3:

Happily

EVER AFTER

We Went to Couples Therapy

AFTER FIGHTING IN FRONT OF THEIR DAUGHTER ONE TOO MANY TIMES, THIS WRITER AND HER HUSBAND SOUGHT OUT A RENOWNED MARRIAGE THERAPIST. THEY GOT TOUGH LOVE AND SO MUCH MORE

BY JANCEE DUNN

There is this amazing guy from Boston, a friend confided in me.

You have an excruciating session with him where he drills down to your problems really fast, then sets you both straight. It's not cheap. And you need to have very, very thick skin. But he stopped us from getting divorced.

I frequently write about relationships for magazines, so I have long known about Terry Real. A family therapist and founder of the Relational Life Institute in Arlington, Mass., Real is a vociferous advocate of moving men and women beyond tired traditional gender roles. Famously blunt, he's an East Coast version of Dr. Phil, sans mustache and Texas twang. Real's specialty is working with couples on the brink of divorce whom no one else has been able to help, sort of a Memorial Sloan Kettering for marriage. Clients, among them celebrities and CEOs, fly to Boston from all over the country for his dramatic relationship overhauls—and pay $800 an hour for the privilege. I reason that a bracing session with him would be the perfect jump start.

Tom and I seat ourselves in his waiting room, leafing distractedly through the magazines on the coffee table.

Just then, the office door swings open and we leap up, almost knocking heads. The Man from Boston.

"Hi," he says, extending his hand. Tall and attractive, with penetrating blue eyes, Real looks to be in his early 60s and possesses a droll warmth that puts us slightly more at ease. He leads us to a wood-paneled office done in soothing greens, browns and blues.

Then he looks at us unblinkingly over his reading glasses. "I always start with the same question," he begins. "This is a lot of money and you've come a long way. What are your hopes? What would a grand slam look like?"

We explain our situation: At least a few times a week, we fight about child care, housework and money, often in front of our 6-year-old, Sylvie. I yell at Tom, and he shuts me out; it is grinding us down and worrying our daughter.

"Sylvie jumps to my defense, and I'm often the one who did something wrong," adds Tom, turning to me. "Maybe that's because you're more, uh . . ."—he searches for a word that will not offend—"vocal?"

Real looks at me. "See, Sylvie will side with him as a way of ameliorating your anger. She's pleading his case to you—'Mom, don't be mad at him.' But it does set up an alliance. And yeah, it's gotta stop." He stops talking and peers at me. "You look sad."

To my profound discomfort, sudden tears are coursing down my cheeks. "I want to be kinder to Tom," I say, snuffling. "But I also want him to do more work around the house and not leave it all to me."

I tell him that Tom has just taken a bike trip through the Italian countryside for 10 days on a magazine assignment. When he came home, he was jet-lagged, so for the ensuing two days, I was once again a single parent as he slept all day. So when he was awake, I yelled.

Real nods. "I got news for ya," he says. "I'm on your side."

I stop in the midst of blowing my nose. "Wait, what? You are?" Real glares at Tom over his reading glasses. "You want to go away for 10 days, biking through the countryside and having pasta at night? You come home, you're there for the kid, and your wife's off her feet." "But—" Tom puts in weakly.

"—I tell you this as somebody who had little kids myself," Real barrels on. "I talk to men all the time and say, 'If you're away from your wife and kids, working, even if it's wall-to-wall work and you come home and you're dog-tired, too bad. If anything, you have to be super thoughtful, because it's really hard to be home with the kids alone."

My triumph must be visible on my face, because Real stops me with a sharp look. "Not that you have a right to behave the way you behaved," he barks. "If he goes away on a trip, don't give it to him and then piss on it on the way out the door. I call that 'peeing on the gift'!"

Real asks me my most pressing issue, and I tell him it's my temper. "I hate myself after I yell," I say.

Real shrugs. "Well, that's useless."

"And I think I get too defensive too quickly, because I'm being yelled at," says Tom. "If I think it's not a major issue, I almost just want to provoke her. So I shut down."

"I will say this," says Real. "Volatile women generally don't feel heard. So you get into: Can you hear me now? *What about now?* That's not going to get you heard. The reciprocal piece of this, Tom, is your walling off and passive aggression. It's a way of expressing your anger by what you don't do. And it's provocative; it actually escalates things."

I tell Real that we almost never fought before we became parents, and he laughs. "Listen, you put a kid in the mix, and then there's this negotiation. That's normal, to some degree. But then throw in your anger and resentment"—he points to me—"and your selfishness and preciousness"—the finger moves to Tom—"and the more angry you get, the more selfish and withdrawn you get. It needs to be nipped in the bud. It's a toxic, self-reinforcing loop that begins to eat away at everything that's good between the two of you." He shakes his head. "You do this pattern for 15, 20 years and you turn into the couples I see who are at the end of this, who are about

I tell the therapist that we almost never fought before we became parents, and he laughs.

to leave. Forty-three percent of couples divorce." (In fact, while the national divorce rate has remained steady since the 1980s, it has doubled for those over 50—when parenting duties are winding down, or over.)

Back to our toxic, self-reinforcing loop. "I feel like I do so much for Tom," I begin. "I bake for him, I—"

"Yeah, yeah, you're very cherishing," Real says. "We get it."

"But before Sylvie was born, I did all the cooking," Tom interjects. "Now Jancee does. How did that happen?"

"Also, I am in charge of Sylvie every day after school," I put in. "That's what I wanted to do. But if I have a deadline and ask occasionally for Tom to take over, he usually refuses. He guards his time."

Tom nods. "My instinctive reaction is no," he admits.

Real frowns. "But she's the after-school mom and the cook and the cleaner-upper," he says. "That would be fine if she didn't work, but not if you're both working. What I see happening with guys is 'Don't mess with me—I need sleep and R&R so I can fight the dragons for my family.' But she's fighting the dragons now, too."

He leans forward. "Tom, what you're not getting, and this is true for most men I see, is that it is in your interest to move beyond your knee-jerk entitlement and to take good care of your wife, so she isn't such a raving lunatic all the time."

Real lists three reasons why men tend to stonewall: They feel that they need to fix the woman's negative experience, and when they can't, they're caught in a "frustrated freak-out." They feel entitled. And no one educated them on how to handle feelings. "Boys are taught to dampen emotions at the age of 3 or 4," he says.

And this suppression continues through adulthood. Marriage researcher John Gottman found that during fights, men are more likely than women to experience diffuse physiological arousal, or DPA, as the body responds to the stress with a "fight or flight" response. This reaction makes a person feel "flooded": the heart beats uncomfortably fast, blood pressure soars, and people have trouble processing information, solving problems or even listening. (If a subject's heart was beating over 100 beats a minute, with some rocketing alarmingly to 168, Gottman found that they were literally not able to hear the other person.) Not only do men tend to experience DPA more than women, but their heart rate stays escalated for a longer period of time and takes longer to return to normal.

To my profound discomfort, tears are coursing down my cheek. "I want to be kinder to Tom."

Real asks Tom if he tends to suppress his emotions during conflict, and he nods. "I think it's easier to have a release when, say, you're driving and someone cuts you off and you flip out."

Real laughs. "Men who won't cry at a funeral will cry at the friendly-dinosaur movie." Then he gets serious again. "So, the best way to make your wife feel heard is to lean into it and disarm her, rather than stonewall her and have a three-hour fight. There are easy ways to do this. It works to say, 'You're unhappy; let me hear what you're talking about,' instead of going away. Then she feels heard, and they render you a nicer guy to live with."

"I will do the work," says Tom solemnly.

I snap back into focus as Real looks at me. "I'm telling you point-blank that this is a good guy, and I'd be shocked if he didn't come through for you," he is saying. "So relax. Trust him."

Well, I think, that was worth the money. What is it, five o'clock? Must be around quitting time. Maybe Italian for dinner?

Then Real turns my way.

"Now," he says, "let's talk about your temper." Uh-oh.

Adapted from the book *How Not to Hate Your Husband After Kids*, by Jancee Dunn.

Money Moves All Couples Should Make

HOW YOU HANDLE YOUR FINANCES AFFECTS HOW HAPPY YOU ARE IN YOUR MARRIAGE. USE THESE FINDINGS TO GROW YOUR RELATIONSHIP—AND YOUR NET WORTH

BY DAN KADLEC WITH KERRI ANNE RENZULLI

Married 38 years, Ron and Carol Beck are the picture of financial compatibility: they split the money chores (he pays the bills, she invests), decide together on big purchases (like their new Corvette) and align their savings goals (retirement has long been No. 1). But the San Jose couple haven't always been so fiscally united.

Unlike many young couples today, they didn't discuss money before marrying. So just months after taking their vows, they took their lumps. One day Ron came home with papers for Carol to sign. It was the first she'd heard of the $35,000 rental property he planned to buy. "We had a huge argument," recalls Carol, 65, a community college counselor. What upset her most was not that their mortgage payments would go up 50% but that Ron acted without her. "I should have been part of the process," she says.

"I knew I overstepped, and I haven't done it since," says Ron, 65, who retired last year from a job as an educational technology supervisor. That night the couple resolved to always act together on major money decisions.

The Becks figured out early on just how critical it is to work as a team when it comes to finances. And a recent study by *Money* underscores the lesson. The poll—which compares the perceptions and behaviors of 500 millennials and 500 boomers when it comes to their relationships and money—reveals distinct dif-

ferences in their approaches to financial matters. But one theme crosses generations: couples who are in sync on saving and budgeting feel more financially secure, argue less about money and have hotter sex lives. In other words, financial synchronicity can help you achieve not only greater financial stability but greater marital satisfaction.

"The secret to being a happy couple is financial compatibility," affirms David Bach, author of *Smart Couples Finish Rich*. The five moves that follow should help you strengthen your union and your finances.

1. Get financially naked with each other

Katy Klein and her fiancé, Charles Hagman, both 30, began opening up about salaries, savings and student loans just nine months into dating. The topics came up naturally as the Seattle couple figured out their plans for attending a pal's wedding. "Some of our friends were going early and renting a home by the beach," says Klein, who works in PR. "So we had a conversation about whether that was in our budget, which spurred other conversations." Hagman, a software engineer, had intended to dig into those issues anyway. But for Klein, it was new terrain. Now that she's done so, however, she says that financial transparency has set a solid foundation for their marriage.

Experts would agree. "Couples have less conflict about money when they share information," says Terri Orbuch, a Detroit family therapist and the author of *5 Simple Steps to Take Your Marriage from Good to Great*. Knowing where you stand and what you want to accomplish builds trust and a sense of teamwork. Plus, getting on the same page gives you a better shot at hitting your goals, she says. Thus, it's crucial for all couples to open their books.

Money's poll suggests that couples are on board with baring all. When it comes to what should be discussed before marriage, boomers and millennials agree that it should include debt (78% of both generations), savings goals (69% and 74%, respectively) and amount saved (63% and 56%).

Yet other research suggests that few married couples truly practice transparency. A few years back, an American Express poll found that 91% of people avoid money talks with their partner. Worse, among adults in a relationship, 1 in 3 acknowledges lying to his or her partner about money, the National Endowment for Financial Education found.

How to do it

Choose a happy moment. Start the transparency conversation around a positive event. "Finances are much easier to talk about when you are flush and happy," says Mary Claire Allvine, a financial planner in Atlanta and the author of *The Family CFO*. "And opening up in good times makes it easier to talk about money when life changes for the worse."

Go full frontal. Crack open a bottle of wine and open your books. Begin by making a net-worth statement. This summary of assets and liabilities gives you a framework for addressing your common goals (see the next section). It can also help you uncover flaws in your strategy, like debt growing as fast as savings. Use an online net-worth calculator like the one at Bankrate.com or an Excel spreadsheet. Plan to update your numbers quarterly.

If you have the energy, make a list of monthly expenses—review the past few months of bank and credit card statements—so you know where money is going. Or upload your accounts to an online money-management tool like Quicken or Mint, says Miami financial planner Ashley O'Kurley.

Find out your mate's musts. Setting goals together begins with understanding your partner, says Patrick Wallace, a financial planner with Higher Strata Wealth Management in Hurst, Texas. He suggests you both answer these questions: What are the three most important money lessons you learned growing up? What are your three biggest money worries? What are your three biggest goals? What are the three most important ways you want to use money to leave a legacy? "Your goals may still be in conflict," says Wallace, "but it will be easier to compromise."

Narrow your common objectives to three—more than that, and you'll have trouble making headway on any. Don't just

stop at setting the goals; also make a plan to reach them. For retirement, see move No. 2; for debt, see No. 4.

2. Don't ignore the elephant in the room

There's no question that couples need to plan for retirement. In fact, since amassing the requisite amount of money will take time, retirement should typically be first on the list of priorities. "When it comes to goals, everything else comes next," says Elizabeth Grahsl, a financial planner in Dallas.

Some 79% of millennials and 91% of boomers in *Money*'s survey say they are in agreement with their partner on saving for retirement. But *Money* also found that, among people who are married or living with a significant other, 1 in 10 boomers and 4 in 10 millennials don't know their partner's retirement account balance; 14% of boomers and 40% of millennials don't know when their partner plans to retire. The costs of not being aligned are substantial: you could end up with less than you need at the finish line.

How to do it

Know your retirement wish lists. Since the amount of savings you need depends on your wants, create a "vision plan" together, says Brad Klontz, a financial psychologist and the author of *Mind over Money*. Write down at what age you want to retire, where you want to live and what you expect your life to look like. Do you want to stay put, downsize ... sail around the world? "Come to the table with your dreams," Klontz says. "Where you agree, it will be easy to adjust your finances, because you are excited."

Do a reality check. First, are you saving enough for the life you want? Check what your nest egg is on track to produce in annual income with T. Rowe Price's Retirement Income Calculator. Also figuring into the equation are Social Security benefits, which make up 38% of income for the average retiree. One way to maximize benefits is to "file and suspend." The higher earner files, then immediately defers benefits to let them grow (they rise 8% for every year you delay between full retirement age and 70). Assuming the lower earner is at full retirement age, he or she can then claim a spousal benefit, deferring his or her own benefit, which will also rise in the meantime. As you near retirement, run this and other basic scenarios using the benefits planner at ssa.gov or more detailed ones at maximizemysocialsecurity.com ($40).

Create a holistic plan. Make sure you're acting as a team when it comes to saving and investing. If you're a two-income household, you probably have access to two 401(k)s, for total annual tax-deferred savings of $36,000, or $48,000 if you're both 50-plus. Stash at least enough in each to get the full company matches. If you can't max out, sign up for automatic increases as your pay rises. You also want to think of your portfolio as one, and make sure you don't have overlap or overexposure in your mix. The Instant X-ray tool at Morningstar.com can help you figure this out. As a general rule, the percentage of your portfolio in stocks should be equal to 110 minus your age; the rest should be primarily in bonds. But if one or both of you have a traditional pension, you could lower the bond allocation, since the guaranteed income allows you to take more risk.

3. Tackle the biggest source of tension

Ira Cohen and his wife, Lisa, have been married for 34 years, and they are the first to admit that they are financial opposites. "She's a 'Let's live for the moment' person, and I err on the side of caution," says Ira, a mutual-fund executive. That created a conflict when the Sugar Land, Texas, couple remodeled their kitchen several years ago. Lisa was insistent on a $1,500 warming drawer that Ira didn't think was necessary. The couple bickered, then "I overrode him and bought it anyway," says Lisa, a high school administrator. He wasn't happy but finally succumbed. "If she is that passionate about this, am I really going to fight and scream over it?" he says.

Money found that 70% of couples argue about money, putting it ahead of conflicts over chores, sex or snoring. What's more, money fights are the only common spats correlated to divorce: couples who fight about money weekly are 52% more likely to divorce than those who argue about money monthly, according to a study by Jeffrey Dew, an associate professor at Utah State University.

Money's survey identified the No. 1 source of conflict as "spending too much on frivolous purchases." A partner's frugality is another major trigger, in the top five for both generations. This classic spender-saver tension can be bad for your marriage and can also be deleterious for your finances.

How to do it

Allow bandwidth on smaller stuff. Spenders feel oppressed by savers watching them like hawks (which may explain why American Express found that 33% of men and 40% of women have hidden purchases from partners). Savers get anxious every time they see their spouses swipe a card. To overcome this tension, automate savings so that those funds are never in question. Also take a cue from the 54% of millennials and 51% of boomers who think spouses should keep some money separate. Klontz says you'll both feel freer if you set up his-and-her discretionary spending accounts about which you ask no questions. To prevent conflicts on joint accounts, set a spending cap, above which each of you has to clear purchases with the other.

Audit yourselves: Record every expense and talk about your findings. Flash-point budgeting can help you uncover cash leaks.

4. Torpedo the silent marriage killer

Two in 10 boomers and millennials say they fight about credit card debt, making this one of the five most common conflicts for both groups. Among the older generation, 61% find excessive debt unattractive. On the surface,

Gen Y seems less concerned about debt, with just 41% saying it's a turnoff. But that's deceiving. Millennials, sometimes called "generation debt," are so weighed down by student loans that many just accept debt as a condition of being young.

In any case, the impact of debt on relationships is undeniable: "It is a silent killer, chipping away at your self-confidence," says psychologist Kathleen Gurney, author of *Your Money Personality*. In fact, Utah State professor Dew found that marital satisfaction is correlated with assets, so that as debt increases, happiness wanes. A big IOU, of course, also stands in the way of your goals. Case in point: More than 70% of young adults say student loans keep them from saving, a National Foundation for Credit Counseling poll found.

The good news is "as couples experience success paying down debt," says Gurney, "they start to see themselves and their partners differently, and the arguing ends."

How to do it

Open with someone's misfortune. Got debt that's burning a hole in your goals? Again, it helps to use a life event to spur the conversation, but in this case a negative one can have more impact. Particularly if one or both of you have been avoiding facing facts, "a soft-and-fuzzy approach won't get results," says Bruce McClary of the National Foundation for Credit Counseling. You might bring up the issues your brother has faced since being downsized, noting how if it had happened to you, your debt might make it tough to respond.

Create a pay-down plan jointly. In *Money*'s survey, 70% of millennials and 77% of boomers say properly managing debt repayment makes for a healthy relationship. Indeed, a systematic approach is the best way to erase balances, says McClary. Some people start with the highest-rate credit cards, to reduce the total interest paid, then move on to other debt. An alternative tack is to start with the smallest balances to enjoy early success.

American Express found that 33% of men and 40% of women have hidden purchases from their partner.

5. Keep tiny tiffs from escalating

Let's face it, even if you two follow all these steps, you'll still occasionally argue about money. How you handle the disagreements is what matters most. A Fidelity survey found that 38% of money arguments are never resolved in a way that makes both people happy. And no wonder—some 16% of millennials and 15% of boomers in *Money*'s poll say they resort to the silent treatment; 12% of millennials and 8% of boomers say someone walks away.

That's not good for your marriage or your money. Not talking about the problem compounds the stress and makes it more likely the argument will recur, says Kim Olver, a relationship coach and the author of *Secrets of Happy Couples*. Plus, leaving the situation unresolved can put stress on your finances. "Do you want to be right?" Olver asks. "Or do you want a strong union? That takes compromise."

How to do it

Acknowledge the argument. Don't go more than 24 hours before touching base with your partner. Consider starting with an apology even if you don't think you need to. You might say, "Honey, I'm sorry I pushed back when you mentioned buying a new car. Can we set aside time to talk more about it?"

Focus on the fear, not the fight. Klontz suggests that before meeting, you each write down the money worry prompting the argument, then meet. The rules: One person talks uninterrupted about his or her fears, avoiding blame. The other must repeat back what was said. Then switch and repeat.

After Carol Beck blew up at Ron about the condo, the couple sat down and talked it through. "He explained to me why he thought it was a good decision." She agreed to sign the papers. "After the property got rented, I relaxed a bit and saw that Ron was right," she says. "Now we talk about everything together. We handle investments very differently than we did that time."

In-Law Management

HELP, OUR FAMILIES KEEP MEDDLING IN OUR LIVES! SOUND FAMILIAR? TAKE THIS ADVICE FOR KEEPING RELATIONS SANE AND STRIFE-FREE

BY REBECCA SAMPLE GERSTUNG

Preserving family harmony with both sets of parents requires a skillful mix of frankness and tact—especially in scenarios like those that follow. And while it's ideal for you and your partner to address major issues with each set of parents as a unit ("We feel ..."), there are some occasions when you must fend for yourself.

Your in-laws always offer unsolicited advice on how to raise your children

SOLUTION: "The best response is 'That's a good idea.' That way, you aren't committing," says Pauline Wallin, a psychologist in Camp Hill, Pa. "On the other hand, you shouldn't automatically reject advice just because it's from your in-laws." They may have a wealth of knowledge to offer (after all, they raised the man or woman you love). Consider how the advice would sound if it came from your best friend. You might also stave off trouble by asking for advice, even if you don't necessarily intend to follow it. Most likely, your in-laws just want to feel involved. In any case, "politely ask that, when they offer advice, they express it as an opinion, not as criticism, which undermines the role of the parents," say Bob Murray, a psychologist, and Alicia Fortinberry, a psychotherapist, the co-authors of *Raising an Optimistic Child*.

Your mother-in-law criticizes your housekeeping skills

SOLUTION: While you may be tempted to enlist your husband in this scenario, it's often better to respond to your mother-in-law directly, since your husband may not feel that this is a battle worth waging and thus may avoid the discussion altogether, says Terri Apter, a psychologist at the University of Cambridge. Be honest. If housekeeping isn't a priority for you, go ahead and tell her, say Liz Bluper and Renée Plastique, the pseudonymous authors of *Mothers-in-Law Do Everything Wrong: M.I.L.D.E.W.* But if her complaints seem unsubstantiated or become an incessant refrain, there could be deeper issues at work. "What seems like a small point may not be," Apter says. "She may not just be saying, 'There is too much dust here' but implying that you're not the kind of woman you should be." Before you tell her where she can stick her dust bunnies, though, keep in mind that she may be unaware of the problem. "People often don't realize that what they're doing is hurting someone," says Beverly Freid, the creator of Motherinlawstories.com, a support-group website. Clue your mother-in-law in, Freid advises, by saying something like "I truly appreciate your concern, but you might not realize that you're hurting my feelings when you make comments about the dusty bookshelves."

Both sets of parents want you to visit them during the holidays

SOLUTION: If you find yourself celebrating every holiday twice—at the expense of your time, budget and waistline—it may be time to compromise. Decide with your husband on a schedule that gives both families equal time, and let everyone know. Try alternating holidays yearly. And don't make false promises. If you don't intend to go to the holiday potluck, don't lead your in-laws to think otherwise; it could cause resentment. Be straight from the start. Still getting

TOP 3 REASONS IT'S ROCKY

Tensions among in-laws often arise from an inescapable fact of extended-family life. As psychologist Terri Apter puts it, "You don't choose your in-laws; you choose your partner." And this usually means that accommodations are needed in three areas.

1. YOU DON'T KNOW HOW HONEST YOU CAN BE

"With your own parents, you can shout, you can complain, you can say that you're hurt," says Apter. However, "you don't know your spouse's family's rules about what can and can't be said—and that is where much of the stress comes from."

2. ROLES ARE CHANGING

"Parents often feel they ought to be like a tribe's council of elders and that children should come to them for advice," says author Alicia Fortinberry. "The younger couple wants to make it on their own and doesn't want the advice from the in-laws, who then get hurt when advice isn't asked for."

3. YOU HAVE ONLY SO MUCH TIME

When a couple get married, often both sets of in-laws feel the new family is an extension of their own. "A conflict of loyalty occurs, and the in-laws may sense it as competition," says psychologist Bob Murray. " 'You see the other family more than you see ours.' "

grief? Host the gathering in your home and invite both sets of parents to join you.

Your husband's mother does things that show she thinks of him as her little boy

SOLUTION: "Most in-law problems boil down to the intrusiveness of one person and the sensitivity of the other," says Wallin. "How does one person send a message, and how does the other receive it?" While your mother-in-law's actions—buying your husband underwear, say—may well be inappropriate, examine why they bother you. Is it because you feel threatened? Discuss your feelings with your husband—it's his job to tell his mother that he's old enough to manage his life. If her babying gets on your every last nerve, put yourself in her shoes. "Empathy is an important part of any relationship," says Murray. Maybe your mother-in-law is acting this way because she's worried about losing touch with her son. "When you can feel empathy for someone, you won't feel so threatened," points out Wallin.

Your in-laws keep asking when you two are going to have children

SOLUTION: While this is a very personal and potentially annoying question, your in-laws may only be asking because they're excited by the prospect. "Acknowledge their needs by saying, 'I know you want grandchildren,' " says Jeri Kadison, a marriage coach in New York. They probably aren't asking in a judgmental way, and even if they are, you can turn it around by saying, "Don't worry—you'll be the first to know."

When your in-laws visit for the holidays, they expect you to embrace their traditions rather than yours

SOLUTION: If the festivities are at your house, you get to make the rules. It's thoughtful to try to incorporate some of their traditions into yours, especially if there are children involved who could benefit from learning different ways of celebrating. But ultimately, it's your home. Gently communicate this to them beforehand so there are no surprises.

It's obvious that your parents and your in-laws don't get along

SOLUTION: In this case, it may be best for you and your husband to talk to your own sets of parents separately. Tell them that you understand that they're not going to be the best of friends with the other couple but that it will make you and your husband happy if they can at least be civil. When it comes to social settings, it may be better to keep them apart than to deal with the stress of potential bickering. Consider the size of the gathering: If it's a small holiday dinner, you might celebrate on two separate nights. Bigger parties should have enough people that both sets of parents can avoid each other. But keep in mind that they are all adults, even if their behavior suggests otherwise. If it's an important event at which you'd like them to all be present—your child's first birthday, say—you can't, and shouldn't, take responsibility for them. And if you're given an ultimatum ("If they're coming, we're not"), simply reply, "We'll miss you."

Every time they take care of your kids, they ignore your rules

SOLUTION: By disregarding your rules, your in-laws are sending a message to you and your children that they know what's best. You and your husband should let them know that you have firm rules about things such as bedtime and how far your children go on their bikes. Also let them know that when they go against such rules, they are undermining your authority. Putting it in the context of what's best for your kids may help to hammer home the point. "Rules need to be clearly set," says Wallin. "If you say no candy, no playing with toy guns, then none of that can happen. If it does, then don't let your in-laws watch your kids."

Your father-in-law always ends up saying something that upsets your husband

SOLUTION: It may hurt you to see this, but your first reaction shouldn't be to snap back at your father-in-law in your husband's defense. Talk to your husband first and offer support. Then, presenting a united front, the two of you should talk to your father-in-law and lay down some ground rules: "We don't want you to say these things. If you do so, you won't be allowed to visit." In situations where your husband and his father aren't talking at all, play diplomatic mediator. "Don't attack," says Wallin. "Ask your father-in-law for permission to discuss it first: 'Would it be all right if I talked to you about something?' People are more apt to listen when you ask permission first."

How to Actually Sleep Together

SNORING SPOUSE? NEEDY CHILD? PETS IN BED? TIME TO TAKE BACK YOUR REST

BY BROOKE HAUSER

While there's plenty of ink spilled on the subject of sleeping together in the conjugal sense, hardly anyone talks about the nightly trial of trying to sleep together in the actual sense. After all, sharing a space that's, give or take, 60 by 80 inches long may be one of the most intimate experiences a couple can have, but it's also one of the trickiest to navigate.

While many of us toss and turn, one in four pairs sleep in separate beds, according to the National Sleep Foundation. As newlyweds in 2010, musician Kevin Jonas and his wife, Danielle Deleasa, were said to sleep in separate rooms due to his heavy breathing. It's not just celebrities: online home-design companies are seeing an increase in demand for house plans with dual master suites.

For all of us still sharing, the together time just might be worth the struggle. "A lot of big talks and moments of sharing happen when we're lying in bed, away from phones, bills, kids, work and multiple daily distractions," says psychologist Tina B. Tessina. "Cuddling up together and talking quietly is a great perk of married life. Couples who know how to do that, and do it regularly,

fare better than couples who don't."

Turns out a healthy sleep ritual helps us roll with the inevitable ups and downs of married life. A study of newlyweds published in the *Journal of Family Psychology* in 2016 found that marital satisfaction was higher after a good night's sleep than a poor one. It also revealed that, for men in particular, a solid sleep prevents little disagreements from turning into unhappiness with the relationship.

Here are some tips to take to bed.

Mismatched schedules

"I wish that dating services, like Match.com, asked people sleep questions," says Michael Breus, a clinical psychologist who is also known as the Sleep Doctor. "When people are learning more about each other, sleep preferences can be a very big persuasion point."

Still, there are bound to be differences. You're trying to sleep, but your spouse wants to read in bed. Or maybe he's in the next room watching a movie, and the volume is too high. A 2016 report that reviewed many studies on couple sleeping found that night-owl behavior is more common in men, and women are more likely to be disturbed by their partner's actions (like going to the bathroom in the middle of the night). Sometimes the best solutions are the obvious but overlooked ones. "If one person likes to read late, instead of using a bedside table lamp, I'll have them buy a book light," Breus says. "If one partner is extremely noise-sensitive, try getting a white-noise machine."

Another common problem is that one person wants to cuddle, and the other isn't ready to go to bed. In that case, "it depends upon the preferences of the person who's going to bed first," Breus says. For example, does the sleeping spouse want to snuggle or simply to be undisturbed by the night owl at 1 a.m.? If the former, Breus suggests that the night owl offer to go to bed early three times a week. (He can always get up again later.) Creating a schedule is "just a way to compromise, to half-and-half it," Breus says. The rest of the week, the night owl can hoot away.

Fun fact: Married couples tend to be awake and asleep at the same time about 75% of the time, according to a study published in the journal *Sleep*. It also found that the happier the wife is with the relationship, the more in sync the couple's sleep schedules are.

Snoring solutions

If you've ever recorded your partner's snoring at night to catch him in the act, you are probably married to one of the 37 million Americans who regularly snore. "We know that if somebody is sleeping next to a snoring bed partner, they will lose approximately one hour of sleep per night just based on those disruptions," says Breus, who is also a fellow of the American Academy of Sleep Medicine (AASM).

Take Shelby Van Voris and her husband, a soldier who fought in Iraq. When he returned in 2008, he developed sleep apnea—a condition in which breathing stops and starts during the night—and it interrupts her rest more than his. Having dozed on cots and floors and in helicopters before, now "he sleeps like a rock," says Van Voris "He's grateful just to have a bed. I could be belly dancing, and he would not be bothered." But she had gotten accustomed to sharing a bed with just her two dogs. "All of a sudden there's this lump," she says of her husband, "and he comes home snoring! The noise was horrendous—I wouldn't wish that on anybody."

In the U.S., approximately 40% of men and 24% of women are habitual snorers. And according to the AASM, obstructive sleep apnea affects more than 29 million men and women, most of them undiagnosed, making it a hidden health crisis. While not all snorers have the disorder, it's important to determine the specific problem to find the right solution. For instance, if your mate does suffer from sleep apnea, he can be treated with an oxygen-supplying CPAP machine so you can both get a better night's rest.

The happier the wife is with the relationship, the more in sync the couple's sleep schedules are.

Little wanderers

Angelina Jolie once told *Vanity Fair* that she and Brad Pitt let their six children pile into their enormous bed for "family sleep." Of course, most people don't have a nine-foot bed or custom-made sheets, and even Jolie admitted that co-sleeping with the kids left Mommy and Daddy "very tired the next morning." (And, in their case, the ritual didn't seem to lead to long-term happiness either.)

Although co-sleeping is a common practice around the world, research has shown that there's a correlation between family sleep and family stress, particularly for women. According to a recent Penn State study, mothers who co-slept with their children past six months suffered more fragmented sleep and reported less marital satisfaction, while fathers who co-slept were not as disrupted or dissatisfied.

In Brooklyn, Gabrielle Balkan goes to sleep by 10:30 p.m., but she is awakened throughout the night: first by her husband, Aaron (a night owl), and then by one of their 6-year-old twin daughters, who has been crawling into their bed when she feels itchy or stuffed-up. "I'm on the edge of the bed anyway, hanging on by a thread, but when she gets into bed, I have even less room, and Aaron is oblivious," says Gabrielle, who often gets up and goes to the twins' room, where she cuddles with her other daughter in the bottom bunk bed before moving to the top bunk. "In the course of the night, I've slept in all three beds!"

As frustrated as parents feel in the middle of the night, Breus advises them to look at the situation the next day with fresh eyes. If your child is routinely getting out of bed, he says, "there should be a cause, and a remedy." Breathing difficulty may be due to enlarged adenoids, which can be removed. Itchy skin may need moisturizer or even cortisone cream before bedtime. If there's not a health issue at play, though, the best cure may be good old-fashioned bribery. Breus used Hot Wheels cars to get his own son to stay in bed through the night, he says: "It works like a charm."

Four-legged friends

According to a recent survey by the American Kennel Club, nearly half of all dog owners let their dog sleep in bed with them. While cuddling up with Rover can be comforting, Tessina encourages mindfulness. "Be careful not to use pets to create distance between you," she says. "Your marriage won't survive if your intimacy doesn't." Her warning calls to mind the classic scene in the comedy *Best in Show* in which a couple and their pet visit a marriage therapist because the pooch is despondent after catching them in the act.

Invest in a good night's rest

The Great Temperature War—it's a battle for countless spouses. In the summer, she cranks the AC; he hates the blowing. He wants the windows open instead, but she has allergies. In the winter, "I definitely sleep cooler, and Aaron sleeps hotter," says Gabrielle, who has gotten used to dressing warmly, sometimes wearing a hat to bed. "Last night, I tried to cuddle with Aaron, and he was like, 'I'm just too hot and sweaty.' "

Sound familiar? If you and your partner run hot and cold, consider investing in products

BEDFELLOWS THROUGH THE YEARS

Who said soul mates have to be bedmates? Here's a brief history of the co-sleeping habits of some celebrated couples, in real life and onscreen

16TH CENTURY

QUEEN ELIZABETH I

Historian Anna Whitelock reported, "Elizabeth was never alone, and in or adjacent to her bed she also had a sleeping companion." An insomniac who was scared of the dark, Elizabeth remained unmarried and chose female bedmates, Whitelock says: "Sharing a bed with a sleeping companion of the same sex was a common practice at the time, providing warmth, comfort and security."

1930S

NICK AND NORA CHARLES

In the 1934 movie *The Thin Man*, married sleuths Nick and Nora Charles shared a king-size bed, but two years later a stringent censorship guide known as the Hays Code forced them to sleep in split singles.

1949

QUEEN ELIZABETH II AND PRINCE PHILIP

In *Elizabeth the Queen*, Sally Bedell Smith quotes Her Majesty's cousin on Elizabeth and Philip's separate bedrooms: " 'In England, the upper class always have had separate bedrooms. You don't want to be bothered with snoring or someone flinging a leg around. Then when you are feeling cozy, you share your room sometimes. It is lovely to be able to choose.' "

1950S

LUCY AND RICKY RICARDO

On *I Love Lucy*, Lucy and Ricky (played by real couple Lucille Ball and Desi Arnaz) had single beds due to the Hays Code, which also outlawed the word "pregnant." At least in English: in a nod to Arnaz's Cuban roots, Lucy shared her baby news in an episode called "Lucy Is Enceinte."

like OppoSheets, which are half-cotton and half-flannel so one of you can stay cool while the other is toasty, or ChiliPad Dual Zone, a mattress pad with a temperature-control system you can each customize.

Good night and good luck

When it comes to co-sleeping, there are lots of ways couples can accommodate each other, but if the tossing and turning continues and you think a sleep disorder may be the cause, it's smart to visit a board-certified sleep doctor.

Since having her husband's sleep apnea diagnosed, Van Voris has upgraded to a king-size bed and bought a CPAP machine. Still, she says, "We have accepted that sometimes we don't sleep in the same bed. We also accept that there are time-out moments when one of us needs a whole lot of sleep and to be left alone: door closed, towel stuffed under the door, earplugs in." She adds that she is mainly thankful to have her husband back home after more than a year at war. "If the only aftereffect is the snoring, then that's minimal. I'll take it," she says. "He's alive."

1960S

MIKE AND CAROL BRADY

In *The Brady Bunch,* Mike and Carol Brady famously cozied up, but they weren't the first TV couple to share a bed. In addition to the real-life spouses on the early sitcom *Mary Kay and Johnny*, Fred and Wilma beat them to the punch on *The Flintstones*.

21ST CENTURY

AVERAGE AMERICANS

In 2007, the National Association of Home Builders predicted that 60% of custom-built homes would feature dual master bedrooms by 2015. The recession put a crimp in those plans for many people, but they can thank a tough economy for bringing them closer.

CAM AND MITCHELL ON *MODERN FAMILY*

ABC's prime-time sitcom, which first aired in 2009, broke ground by showing America a gay couple in all kinds of ordinary intimate moments, including in bed.

KATIE HOLMES AND TOM CRUISE

Before they split in 2012, Katie Holmes reportedly kicked Tom Cruise to the "snore room" in their house to get her beauty sleep.

RESPECTING THE PAST

A traditional Shinto wedding ceremony takes place at Tokyo's Meiji Shrine, which honors the spirits of 19th-century emperor Meiji and his wife, Empress Shoken.

Tying the Knot

THERE ARE A WORLD OF WAYS FOR TWO PEOPLE TO BECOME ONE

BY ANDRÉA FORD

ANCIENT WAYS

In Gansu Province of northwest China, a bride, dressed in the traditionally colorful garb of the minority ethnic Yugur group, is taught how to make milk tea by the groom's family.

LOVE ME TENDER

A German couple marry in one of the many unconventional wedding chapels of Las Vegas—the so-called Wedding Capital of the World—with the help of an Elvis impersonator.

MAKING HISTORY

Ray Durand and Dale Shields are photographed after marrying in Manhattan's city clerk office on July 24, 2011, the day New York began performing same-sex marriages.

DIVING IN

As the celebrant performs the ceremony from behind the glass, James Oliver weds Kathryn O'Connor while immersed in the ocean-reef tank of the London Aquarium.

BEHIND THE VEIL

An ultra-Orthodox Jewish bride looks at her groom from behind a gauzy curtain during a dance ritual at their wedding in Mea Shearim, one of the oldest and most insular neighborhoods of Jerusalem.

TAKING THE PLUNGE

Rick Harker and Marlene Hoar rappel down the side of a Vancouver skyscraper as part of their 2009 wedding ceremony, which doubled as a charity event benefiting children with disabilities.